I Hear You

I Hear You

REPAIR COMMUNICATION BREAKDOWNS,

NEGOTIATE SUCCESSFULLY,

AND BUILD CONSENSUS . . .

IN THREE SIMPLE STEPS

Donny Ebenstein

AMACOM

American Management Association

New York • Atlanta • Brussels • Chicago • Mexico City • San Francisco
Shanghai • Tokyo • Toronto • Washington, D.C.

Bulk discounts available. For details visit:
www.amacombooks.org/go/specialsales
Or contact special sales:
Phone: 800-250-5308
E-mail: specialsls@amanet.org
View all the AMACOM titles at: www.amacombooks.org

This publication is designed to provide accurate and authoritative information in regard to the subject matter covered. It is sold with the understanding that the publisher is not engaged in rendering legal, accounting, or other professional service. If legal advice or other expert assistance is required, the services of a competent professional person should be sought.

Library of Congress Cataloging-in-Publication Data

Ebenstein, Donny.
  I hear you : repair communication breakdowns, negotiate successfully, and build consensus . . . in three simple steps / Donny Ebenstein.
      pages   cm
  Includes bibliographical references and index.
  ISBN-13: 978-0-8144-3219-8
  ISBN-10: 0-8144-3219-0
  1. Communication in management.   2. Communication in organizations.
3. Interpersonal communication.   4. Interpersonal conflict.   I. Title.
  HD30.3.E24 2013
  658.4'5—dc23
                                                                    2013001923

About AMA
American Management Association (www.amanet.org) is a world leader in talent development, advancing the skills of individuals to drive business success. Our mission is to support the goals of individuals and organizations through a complete range of products and services, including classroom and virtual seminars, webcasts, webinars, podcasts, conferences, corporate and government solutions, business books, and research. AMA's approach to improving performance combines experiential learning—learning through doing—with opportunities for ongoing professional growth at every step of one's career journey.

Printing number

10   9   8   7   6   5   4   3   2   1

Contents

CHAPTER **5**

Looking from the Outside In: Seeing Is Believing   116

CHAPTER **6**

Don't Take It Personally: Understanding It's Not About You   146

Acknowledgments

Like all books, this one could not have been written without the help of many people along the way. I was the fortunate beneficiary of their help; all errors are mine alone.

My training in this field at Harvard Law School was excellent, and I was fortunate to learn from some of the best. I thank my teachers, who helped me enter into this field while still a student, and all of the folks at the Program on Negotiation (PON) with whom I had the pleasure of working.

I would also like to thank the Reginald F. Lewis Foundation for awarding me a fellowship, allowing me to travel to Costa Rica to teach mediation just after my graduation. Although the fellowship itself was modest in both duration and funding, it was hugely important in shaping my decisions; it gave me the confidence and encouragement needed to pursue a career in this field, and for that I am truly grateful.

In the arc of my professional life, I have worked at many different organizations, both in the United States and around the world. Over the past seventeen years I have been blessed to work with many wonderful colleagues, too numerous to name here. Each one helped me learn and grow as a professional, and I am deeply appreciative of their friendship and their wisdom.

The Babylonian Talmud (Ta'anit 7a) quotes Rabbi Hanina on

recognizing those from whom he learned: "I learned much from my teachers, and more from my friends than from my teachers, and from my students, I learned most of all." Clients are not quite students, but I would agree with Rabbi Hanina that we learn most from those we are trying to teach. I thank all of the clients that I have worked with over the years, who shared their challenges with me and allowed me the privilege of working with them on their stuck situations. So much of this book comes from the lessons that my clients taught me.

I would like to thank my agents, Pat and Michael Snell. Despite the many flaws in the initial proposal I sent them, they saw what this book could become and took me on as a first-time author. Pat, I have tried to "show, not tell" at every turn. Writing a proposal that Pat and Michael were satisfied to send to publishers was almost as hard as writing the book itself, and I hope the results speak for themselves.

Betty Rauch gave me valuable advice on how to reach the right audience with this book, and her warmth and humor gave me support along the way.

My parents have been an unwavering source of love and respect, and whatever I have accomplished and will accomplish in my career would not have been possible without the strong foundation they gave me early in life.

My parents-in-law gave me love and support at many key points and have treated me like their very own son in every way.

I also want to thank my sons, Avishai, Noam, and Elitzur, who lent moral support and, like most families, ended up absorbing some of my stress through this process, particularly before important deadlines.

There is one person I want to thank above all others, and that is my wife, Debra. She knew I had this book inside me even before I did, and she supported me in all ways as it moved from a mere idea to a reality. It is no exaggeration to say that without her, I doubt I could have written it at all.

Note to Readers

This book comprises multiple dialogues and examples in which the concepts are applied to specific situations. While the stories come from real-life experiences, they have all been modified. All names and identifying details have been changed to preserve people's privacy, and most cases reflect amalgams of various individuals' similar experiences.

From Conflict to Consensus

In the three years I spent acquiring my degree from Harvard Law School, I learned that I actually didn't want to be a lawyer. Instead of being a gladiator on behalf of my clients, I wanted to help people listen to the other side, communicate more effectively, and resolve their conflicts amicably. If I were successful, they would learn and grow from their difficult situations, avoiding conflict in the future.

Shortly after my graduation, I got the chance of a lifetime, winning a fellowship to intern at a conflict resolution center sponsored by the Supreme Court of Costa Rica. I had been in Costa Rica for less than a week, living in the capital of San José. It was Sunday night when I got a phone call from Gabriela, the training director. A presenter who was scheduled to accompany her on a trip to the south suddenly had to cancel for personal reasons. The team, she explained, was now one presenter short—could I go in his place?

A combination of excitement and terror filled me. I was going to have a chance to teach people about the power of conflict resolution. But was I really ready to do that, in a foreign country and speaking a foreign language? What if I flopped?

"Of course I'll go," I said.

The presentation was taking place in Sierpe, a small tropical town in swamplands near the Pacific coast. The weather was hot, humid, and extremely uncomfortable, and I cursed my American button-down shirt, necktie, and wool dress pants. My stomach was in agony from drinking the water that my American stomach couldn't handle. Sweating and miserable, I made my way over to where the presentation would take place—a concrete floor with three grass walls and a grass roof. Our hosts had set up an overhead projector and some sixty chairs for the audience—but no microphone. The acoustics were terrible; to be heard I almost had to yell.

Despite these obstacles, the presentation was a huge success, flawed Spanish and all. My confidence soared, and I went on to do several more such presentations, as well as actual mediations, in other cities and in San José. Success built on itself, and I returned from Costa Rica determined to build a career in this field. Since then, over the past seventeen years, I have been fortunate to be able to turn my passion into a profession. As I think about how my career began with that presentation, two lessons come to mind.

First, I learned that when I shared a message and taught people skills that I truly believed in, I could be effective in virtually any setting. I have worked successfully as a trainer, mediator, facilitator, consultant, curriculum designer, and coach. I've done so with many different types of populations—senior business executives, teachers, psychologists, army officers, hedge fund managers, social workers, police officers, salespeople, attorneys, school administrators, bankers, judges, and more. I have worked all around the world, including in Latin America, the Middle East, Australia, China, Japan, and throughout Europe.

Second, I realized that the need to answer some basic questions is nearly universal: How can I communicate more effectively? How can I build and improve relationships? How can I resolve conflicts? No matter where people worked or what they did for a living, these were the questions that kept surfacing. The desire for help in these areas is both intense and widespread, and when presented with tools that will help, people respond. I've written this book to help people communicate more effectively, particularly in their most stuck, conflict-ridden situations.

BECOMING YOUR OWN COACH

My first encounter with conflict resolution came while still a law student, mediating in the local small claims court. Small claims cases are disputes where the dollar amounts are typically low (a few hundred dollars) but the emotions are high. They might involve an unhappy customer, an unpaid contractor, feuding neighbors, or even quarrels between family members. The goal of small claims mediation is to help the parties resolve their dispute amicably, without having to go before a judge. There are many benefits to settling a dispute rather than receiving a judgment, including better enforcement of the agreement, saving time, protecting one's reputation, and improving relationships (which can be especially important between neighbors or family members).

I volunteered to become trained as a mediator. In the thirty-two-hour mediation course, we learned many different skills, including how to build rapport with the parties, how to ask questions, how to listen effectively, and how to show empathy.

As I began mediating actual cases, I was amazed to see how this process unlocked what appeared to be intractable conflicts, assisting the parties in reaching a mutually acceptable resolution. I asked myself, "Why is mediation effective? If it was possible to settle the case all along, why didn't it settle before? And if it was not possible previously, what has the mediator done to change that?"

Over time, I came to realize that the mediator played an essential role in fostering mutual understanding. A mediator can listen to each side's perspective, understand and validate that perspective, and simultaneously help each party listen to and understand the other side's perspective. The mediator bridges the gaps in understanding between parties. It is this fostering of mutual understanding, in turn, that unlocks the situation and opens up new possibilities for the parties to communicate with one another and to ultimately think creatively about possible solutions that had not been considered before.

But it's not always practical to call in a mediator. Whether your stuck situation is with a colleague, a subordinate, your manager, an important client, or anyone else, you may not have the luxury of calling in a skilled and neutral outsider to bridge the gaps in understanding. And in those cases, you need to help yourself by becoming your *own* coach, your own outside neutral party. Unilaterally, you can bridge the gaps in perspective, the way a mediator would, and harness the power of mediation to get unstuck all by yourself. This doesn't mean giving in, and it doesn't mean giving up. It just means stepping outside your perspective and looking at your situation from a neutral vantage point. This book provides you with strategies and techniques to do just that.

Chapter One describes the problem of being stuck. We all encounter situations where we don't know how to make things better, making us feel trapped and helpless. The first step is to recognize that you have the power to change things by behaving differently yourself. Even when things seem hopeless, the dynamics of an interpersonal interaction can be changed by just one of the parties doing something differently.

In order to interact differently with your counterparty, you need to find a way to *think* differently. Looking for new words to say isn't the answer; you need to learn to shift your perspective and flex your mind to create new possibilities in how you interact with the other side. This is the subject of Chapter Two. Flexing one's mind, however, is no small feat. Chapter Three describes the barriers to engaging in this process that can get you stuck, and it provides you with some suggestions for how to get past these challenges.

We've all heard similar advice before: Put yourself in the other person's shoes. But to really get it, to truly get unstuck, you need to do more than put yourself in the other person's place. Rather, you need to build your capacity to see different perspectives *at the same time*. A concrete way of visualizing what I am advocating occurred to me one evening while I was sitting in my apartment. I live on the fourth floor of a six-floor apartment building. As anyone who has lived in an apartment knows, noise travels from units above to units below. In our line of apartments, all of the residents are families with small children, and we all make plenty of noise.

On this particular evening, my upstairs neighbors were being quite loud. Their kids were running around, throwing toys, banging, and generally making a huge ruckus. I was becoming quite frustrated and was tempted to go upstairs to complain and say, "You need to keep your kids quieter and be sensitive to your downstairs neighbors."

But I paused. Just then, I heard a loud crash from my kids' room, where a soccer game was in progress. I considered how we sounded to my downstairs neighbors. I'm sure the ruckus that my children were making was just as disturbing to the family that lives under us. If they were to come upstairs and complain, I would probably want to say something like, "Look, kids are noisy, and there is not much that can be done. This is the reality of apartment living."

This experience was an eye-opener for me. I had a moment of clarity, where I realized that there were two legitimate perspectives to this situation—the upstairs perspective and the downstairs perspective. And this is true in any stuck situation: There are multiple justifiable perspectives, different yet valid ways to look at what is going on.

The ability to see both perspectives at the same time helped me to successfully manage my frustration. In this case, it was simple, since I was simultaneously living the experience of both an upstairs and downstairs neighbor, both the victim and the perpetrator of noisemaking. It was therefore much easier to flex my mind and view the noise coming from upstairs through the eyes of the upstairs neighbor, instead of just being annoyed by the thumping from above. It's not that it wasn't noisy; rather, I could understand that they were doing their best, just as I was doing mine.

Three chapters (four, five, and six) together offer a framework for how to shift perspective without losing your own story; that is, how to apply the upstairs–downstairs paradigm to your own stuck situations. There are three different ways of shifting perspective that I recommend, all of which can be used to gain a bird's-eye view of your case. They include telling the other side's story (Chapter Four), learning to see yourself as others see you (Chapter Five), and recognizing how your dynamic is affected by the system or structures in place, rather than just by the personalities involved (Chapter Six.) Using examples and mock dialogues, each of these chapters models how you can achieve the respective shift in thinking. They also provide you with concrete pointers on how you can have a conversation with the other side in the wake of that shift.

Most of the time people become stuck in their own perspective. It's deceptively easy to believe that you've understood another point of view when you've actually failed to understand the other issues at hand. These three chapters will help you make sure that you have successfully flexed your mind—that you really *do* get it. However, sometimes people can have the reverse problem. They become lost in the other side's perspective. Rather than seeing both the upstairs and downstairs positions at the same time, they adopt the other side's narrative in lieu of their own story. Whether this is a common problem for you or merely an occasional challenge, Chapter Seven tackles the question of how to flex your mind without losing your *own* narrative. By this point in the book, you'll have mastered the skill of telling the upstairs and downstairs stories at the same time—and you'll be able to prepare accordingly.

Once you've acquired these skills, you'll need to apply what you have learned to real life. When you are trying to pinpoint what is getting you stuck, and how these various shifts can help you get unstuck in your particular case, it can be useful to engage in role-playing. In Chapter Eight, I define role-playing and highlight the ways it can help you get unstuck. Role-playing can be useful as a diagnostic tool, and it is also essential for preparing you for future—and smoother—interactions with your counterparty.

Flexing your mind in different ways and role-playing your situation will enable you to generate multiple new options that can open the doors to your stuck situation. Chapter Nine delves into the various possibilities that may emerge. You may flex your mind and come up with creative options for making things better. Alternatively, after seeing things differently, you may decide that the status quo works for you and simply tweak it for your own comfort. In some extreme situations, you may decide that leaving the situation is what's best for you. After having flexed your mind, any of these options leads to empowerment, as you will have undergone a process through which you have made a conscious, thorough, and informed decision about what works best for you.

Getting stuck is a fact of life. Difficult situations and difficult people are all around us, and no one, not even the most skilled communicator, can avoid getting stuck 100 percent of the time. While you can't control other people, you *can* control your own behavior. The good news is that the methods outlined in this book will help you alter your situation unilaterally. My hope is that this book will help you to bring out the best version of yourself so that you can cope more skillfully with the difficult situations you will inevitably encounter.

CHAPTER 1

Change Yourself

GOING FROM STUCK TO UNSTUCK

Harriet opened the conversation by saying, "Look, we were quite disappointed with the workshop, and I think this is feedback you need to take seriously." As Harriet detailed her dissatisfaction with the program, John, who managed client relationships for his firm, was fuming inside. All of her criticisms—all of them!—were things he had warned her about ahead of time. She said, "John, the session was too short." John steamed, recalling that when he had inquired about running a longer session, Harriet had said they could not give the topic more time. Harriet continued, saying, "You know, the junior staff was intimidated and didn't want to participate." When John had asked about dividing the group according to seniority, she told him that her marching orders were to keep the junior and senior staff together. And, to make matters worse, she hadn't let John interact with any of her senior managers one-on-one; she had insisted on being part of every phone call and meeting. This meant that John had no opportunity to sidestep Harriet. Her meddling in the design of the workshop had made things much harder and had negatively affected the final outcome.

After delivering all of the negative feedback, Harriet paused, obviously giving John a chance to respond. He wanted to speak up, but he was afraid of antagonizing his client. Now what? John was stuck.

John's situation is one we can all relate to. You find yourself in a dynamic with someone important to you—a client, a manager, a colleague, a family member—where you don't know what to say or do. You may be stumped as to how to respond, afraid of sounding too aggressive, or fearful that being honest will make things worse. The good news is that you are not alone, and that there is something you can do to get unstuck.

DEFINING STUCK SITUATIONS

Being stuck, in this context, is not like being stuck in the mud, unable to move. It's more like being caught in a maze, running in circles, where all of your motion somehow doesn't lead to progress. You just don't know how to respond in a constructive fashion. Not only do you not see how you can make it better, your attempts to make it better just make it worse. You have the feeling that there is simply nothing that could make this situation go differently.

Consider the following example. I was at a party at a friend's house chatting with a woman I had just met. Her name was Wendy, and she asked me what I did for a living. When I told her that I coach people on how to communicate, collaborate, and negotiate more effectively in their most challenging situations, Wendy proceeded to tell me all about a difficult situation she was having with a colleague at work. Kevin, a peer of hers, would always find a way to avoid working late or on the weekends. He managed to duck most difficult assignments, which somehow ended up on Wendy's desk. In general, Wendy felt he was not doing his fair share of the work, and she was left picking up the slack. She tried to politely raise the topic with Kevin, but got nowhere. Wendy asked me for my advice, and we had the following conversation:

Me: What happens when you try to talk to Kevin about sharing the load more evenly?

Wendy: It doesn't go well.

Me: What does he say?

Wendy: He gets defensive. He tells me not to micromanage him, and that it's none of my business what time he goes home.

Me: How do you respond to that?

Wendy: I usually tell him that people perceive him negatively and that it's not good for his reputation to be seen leaving early.

Me: And?

Wendy: He tells me that he is getting his work done, so there is no problem.

Me: Is he right?

Wendy: Yes and no. He is very efficient and does get his work done. But I can also work quickly, and so can other people at the firm. It's not as if people get their work done and then just leave at five o'clock. If you can take on more work, you do. It's only Kevin who leaves so early.

Me: Did you tell him that?

Wendy: Not in so many words. But I did say that everyone is working hard and everyone wants to get home, and he should think about other people's workloads, not just his own.

Me: What about raising the issue with your manager?

Wendy: My manager doesn't care. She said that she tries to balance the load among the team, and she does not monitor what time Kevin leaves, as long as he gets his work done.

Me: And what do you think about that?

Wendy: Well, in principle that makes sense. But it doesn't work in practice. It's not always clear how long something will take. So a project might take two hours or it might take eight hours, and you don't know which until you get deep into it. If something gets done quicker, you can take on more work. And somehow it always seems as if I get the more demanding and time-consuming projects.

Me: Have you said anything to your manager about how projects are assigned?

Wendy: Yes, I did. I mean, I said it sort of indirectly, but I did say something.

Me: What exactly did you say?

Wendy: I asked her how she decided who got which assignment, and she said that there wasn't really any system. She looked at who didn't get any new assignments lately and gave it to them. She didn't seem to appreciate being questioned, so I dropped the subject.

Me: Were you afraid that she would feel you were attacking her?

Wendy: Yes. And she tends to get defensive and sometimes even retaliates against people who "make trouble." I don't want to be the whiner on the team. Besides, it's not as if I can't get the work done; if I have to work late a few nights, so be it.

Me: But it sounds like this situation is making you resentful.

Wendy: Yes, it is. But I have learned that sometimes you can't beat the office politics. I guess I should just recognize that not everyone is going to be a team player and forget about the whole thing.

Wendy was stuck in her situation. She was unhappy with how things were going but felt helpless to change them. I knew she was stuck because she expressed a strong feeling of resignation. The things she had tried didn't improve the situation, but actually made it worse. She had already called it quits and given up on making things better for herself, even though it clearly bothered her enough that she recounted the whole story to a perfect stranger.

In stuck situations, it is natural to give up trying to make it better. As people get more frustrated, they tend to either lash out or withdraw. Sometimes they do both, first lashing out and then withdrawing, disengaging, and ultimately leaving the situation.

The costs of Wendy's frustration and her despair that nothing will make things better are not only borne by her. The company also suffers. As Wendy, a productive contributor to her team, becomes unhappy and resentful, her productivity goes down. There is a significant risk that she will leave the company altogether, and the cost of replacing a skilled employee is high.

This book was written to address these types of "stuck situations." Here are some ways to tell if you are in a stuck situation:

> Are you dissatisfied with what is happening now?

> Do you find yourself in a dynamic that repeats itself? Is there a pattern to what is happening?

> Do you feel powerless to change the situation?

> Are you clueless as to what to do to make it better?

> Did the things you've already tried doing to make the situation get better fail or make it worse?

> Are you resigned to feeling unhappy?

> Do you find yourself thinking that the other person is the worst person in the world?

If so, this book can help you.

FIXING IT BEGINS WITH YOU

While grappling with a stuck situation, the people closest to you are often the ones who make things worse. Why? Because they support you by sympathizing with your feelings, assuring you that it's not your fault, and reinforcing your perception that there is nothing you can do to make things go differently. The "supportive friend" conversation goes something like this:

Wendy: I can't believe I have to work this weekend again.
Supportive Friend: I know.

Wendy: Kevin is such a jerk. He knows just how to maneuver to get out of the toughest assignments. He didn't stay late even one night this week.

Supportive Friend: And you were working such long hours.

Wendy: I know. It's infuriating.

Supportive Friend: Every office has someone like that. There's not much you can do about it.

Wendy: Why doesn't my manager see it?

Supportive Friend: She's probably just lazy. She knows you will get everything done, so why make an issue with Kevin?

Wendy: And she is on a total power trip. God forbid that anyone should criticize her management or how she runs the team.

Supportive Friend: I bet she is threatened by you and knows she can't afford to lose you. You are really good at your job.

Wendy: Well, I am not going to let people treat me this way.

Supportive Friend: You should look for a new place to work.

Wendy's friend wants to be supportive. But not only is she failing to help Wendy; she is actually hurting her. By simply agreeing with Wendy's story and never challenging it, she is making it easier for Wendy to cling to the notion that there is nothing she can do about this situation.

And here is the starting point for our work together in this book: It begins with *you*. You have the power to shift your most stuck situations.

This is a powerful and transformative idea. You can make things better on your own. Just by behaving differently yourself, you can shift your whole dynamic with another person, even when it feels hopeless!

And yet, when I tell this to people, they become defensive. Consider the following exchange, which is the continuation of my conversation with Wendy:

Me: So what are you going to do?

Wendy: I don't know. I don't think there is much I can do. I know you do coaching and try to help people, but some situations are just not fixable.

Me: Do you feel this is one of those situations?

Wendy: Yes.

Let's pause here. Wendy is clearly stuck. She has decided the problem is not fixable, and she's given up. She feels that it is hopeless. Based on what she described so far, do you agree? Is her situation hopeless?

It is hard to tell. But it is much better to err on the side of hopeful, rather than hopeless. We continued as follows:

Me: I think the situation may not be hopeless, Wendy. And I think there's a lot you could be doing to make it better.

Wendy: What do you mean?

Me: I think some of the things you did have contributed to the problem. For example, I don't think you had a constructive conversation with Kevin to talk about this situation. It sounds like you were a bit aggressive in how you raised this topic with him, which made him defensive. It's no surprise, then, that it did not go well.

Wendy: What? I can't believe you are saying it's my fault! I'm the one who is working my tail off all weekend. Kevin is the freeloader who goes home at five o'clock. Why are you blaming it all on me?

What do you think of Wendy's reaction? Did I blame her for the situation? Is this all her fault? Isn't Kevin the one who needs to do things differently?

When I tell people that they can change their stuck situations, they often react as Wendy did. They get defensive, because they feel they are being blamed. They then seek to prove how they are *not* at fault, and how they *can't* do anything to change their stuck situation.

But hold on a minute. I didn't blame Wendy for Kevin's bad behavior. I pointed out that she could have had a more constructive conversation with Kevin about it. That doesn't make the problem her fault.

And here is the good news. If I'm right, and Wendy could have handled the conversation with Kevin differently, then it's possible that she could have elicited a different response from him. It is a wonderful thing to be told that you can change your stuck situation. Wouldn't you want to know that there is something you can do that can make a difference in your dynamic with your manager/colleague/neighbor/spouse/client or whomever else you struggle with, even if the problem was not one you created? Isn't it better for Wendy if she discovers that she is not limited to sucking it up or finding a new job, but she could actually make things better by changing her own behavior?

It's important for me to reiterate that just because you may decide to behave differently does not mean that it's your fault. Fault is a useful concept in a tort lawsuit to show that someone should be held liable to pay damages. But in interpersonal interactions, whether you are at fault doesn't matter in the end. What matters is what can be done to make things better.

Fundamentally, the way to get unstuck in your most stuck situations is by first assuming that you *can* change things by being different yourself. I know people will fight me on this point. And it's not true a hundred percent of the time. There are situations where even if you decide to behave differently it won't be enough to change things (and in Chapter Nine we will address that issue).

But even though there are some relationships that cannot

be repaired, most of the time you can change things by doing something different yourself. Overcoming your own despair and adopting a proactive, optimistic stance that you *can* change things unilaterally is the secret to making a change.

Here's what I said to Wendy:

Me: Let's take a step back. It sounds like you are in a frustrating situation at work right now.

Wendy: Yeah, tell me about it.

Me: And I am not saying it's your fault. Believe me, if I were talking to Kevin right now, or if I were talking to your manager, I would be pushing them to examine their own behavior just as I am pushing you. They are part of the dynamic and bear responsibility for what's going on as well.

Wendy: Okay. I'm glad you see that.

Me: I am simply saying that I believe you can do much more than you have done so far to make it better. And that's not bad news; it is good news.

Wendy: How so?

Me: It's good news because it gives you power and leverage to make a change. You cannot change other people, but you can change yourself. You can't force Kevin to stay at work past five. And you can't force your manager to care. But I believe that if you change yourself, and how you engage with your colleagues and manage these conversations, they will probably respond to you differently. The potential for making things better has yet to be tapped.

Wendy: So coach me. What should I do?

This was the opening I was waiting for. Once Wendy accepted that she could change things, and asked me how to do that, we were halfway there.

Me: Let's start by examining this situation from other points of view. I think there is a lot to this story that you may be missing. It's likely not as hopeless as you think.

Wendy: It's been going on like this for months.

Me: I was thinking that maybe you need to look at things from Kevin's point of view.

Wendy: How?

Me: Well, you told me that Kevin is a fast worker and superefficient. You told me that he works very hard to get everything done so that he can leave at five in the afternoon. Do you know why he does that?

Wendy: He recently had a baby, and since then he has been much more eager to get home.

Me: Is he doing less than other people?

Wendy: Not really. He's not doing less, but he is certainly not doing more, either.

Me: So from his point of view, he is doing just as much work as he was before; he is just working even more quickly so that he can finish earlier. Right?

Wendy: Yes.

Me: Well, if that's the case, it makes sense that he insists the balance of work within the team is fair. It doesn't mean he is right, but at least you can see where he is coming from.

Wendy: But if I get my work done more quickly, I take on more work. That is what I think my manager expects of me.

Me: Another dimension to the situation is the absence of an honest conversation with your manager about this matter. You haven't shared your concerns or your frustrations with her. Why not?

Wendy: I don't feel comfortable raising it.

Me: Then I think that is something you could work on. Besides, from your manager's point of view, the system probably appears to be working fine. Unless you speak up, how will she know that there is a problem?

Wendy: Are you saying this whole situation is my responsibility to fix?

Me: No, not at all. I'm just saying that you have a lot more power to change things than you realize. When we started this conversation, you were resigned that things would never get better. I'm hoping that what we've talked about so far will change your mind on that.

Wendy: How can things get better?

Me: Well, you can decide to talk to Kevin about his work–life balance more directly. Or you can opt to have a more direct conversation with your manager. Finally, you might consider simply changing your own behavior. Rather than taking on more work whenever you can, slow your pace so that you don't become resentful and burnt out. For all you know, your manager might not expect more than that. At the end of the day, knowing you have options on how to respond can be a real game-changer.

I don't know what happened with Wendy in the end. I hope she took some initiative and did something about her problem. But I fear that she did what most of us do—the same things we have been doing until now.

Doing what we have been doing is comfortable. It's familiar. It feels safe. And it's the most natural thing to do—we got this far by following our gut instinct, and that gut instinct is naturally going to tell us to keep on going this way.

But changing the situation starts with changing yourself. This doesn't mean that other people don't also have to change. It doesn't let the other people off the hook. It just means that we need to look first at ourselves and how we can change, because that is where we have the most leverage over the stuck situation. It would be great if we had a magic wand we could wave to make the other person be different. But we don't. In fact, we don't even have a magic wand to wave to make ourselves different. What we do have is the capacity to learn new approaches and the motivation and discipline to apply those new approaches. And this book will give you some techniques you can use once you decide that change is what you want.

Are you ready to commit to this challenge?

WHY BEING DIFFERENT MAKES ALL THE DIFFERENCE

People often struggle to believe in the concept that if they are different, the dynamic will be different. Even once a person moves past the initial defensiveness of feeling blamed, the way Wendy did, it remains a puzzling idea. If the other person is a jerk, how will my behavior make a difference? How can I change my counterpart? He is who he is, right?

Wrong. What is missing is an understanding that *who* the other person is in general is not the same thing as *how* that person is behaving right now. People do have personalities, which are stable traits that describe how any given person tends to behave in various situations. But personality alone doesn't dictate how someone acts. Far from it. How a person is treated by her counterpart is a hugely important variable in how that person responds, regardless of her personality.

Put another way, different situations elicit different responses from us. If someone is rude to me, I am more likely to be rude in return. Conversely, if someone is polite to me, I am more likely to be polite in response. This is the case regardless of whether my natural tendency is toward rudeness or politeness. There are clear differences between people with different personality traits. For instance, when faced with the same situation, aggressive people will react more harshly than timid people do. Yet for any person, aggressive or timid or anywhere in between, how he responds is highly dependent on how he is treated. This is obvious, right? Therefore, when I am dealing with a rude person, I am more likely to get a polite response if I treat that rude person politely. Changing how I behave changes how he behaves, regardless of his personality.

Here is a metaphor to consider: Imagine that I am helping my friend move to a new house, and we are moving his furniture. We are carrying a table from the moving truck into the house, and it's not easy because the table is quite heavy. Now, suppose that I, unilaterally and without consultation, decide to lift the table higher so I can carry it more easily. Will that affect my friend and how he carries his half of the table? Of course it will. And this is true even if I do it without warning and without permission. Because the table is being held by both of us, when one of us moves or shifts, by necessity the other one must move or shift as well. There is no escaping that fact.

In a similar way, when I change how I communicate in my stuck situation, the other person will inevitably react and change how he communicates as well, often in dramatic ways. When I change my part of the dynamic, the other party to the conversation—the other person carrying the burden of that dynamic—will also have to shift.

In Wendy's example, Kevin is who he is, and that is not something she can change. But how he responds to Wendy when they discuss workload, whether he becomes defensive or keeps an open mind, is highly dependent on how Wendy treats him. They are reacting to one another.

Here is an example of how this dynamic could play out in an actual conversation. Andre was a banker who struggled with his manager named Marvin. They were in a high-pressure environment, and whenever things got tense, Marvin would lash out at Andre and yell at him. At a recent client meeting, Andre failed to bring some files that the client had wanted to see. Both Marvin and Andre were embarrassed and upset about disappointing the client, and after the meeting they fought about it. Here was their conversation:

Marvin: I can't believe that you screwed up that client meeting.

Andre: It wasn't my fault.

Marvin: Yes, it was. Stop trying to pass the buck.

Andre: I don't appreciate you blaming me for your own mistakes. You were the one who scheduled the meeting, and I assumed you found out what the client wanted to discuss.

Marvin: It's your job to prepare materials before a client meeting!

Andre: But I can't do my job when you don't tell me important information!

Marvin: I am so tired of fighting with you just to get you to do your job.

This conversation was upsetting for both Andre and Marvin. Marvin attacked Andre, and Andre—understandably—responded defensively. Both of them ended up raising their voices in anger. Andre felt stuck and unable to change things.

Now imagine a conversation where Andre handles himself differently. Andre alone has decided to change his behavior; notice how this changes what Marvin says.

Marvin: I can't believe that you screwed up that client meeting.

Andre: I was upset with how it went as well.

Marvin: It's your job to prepare materials for the meeting. You should have found out which files were needed.

Andre: Look, I'm sorry that I didn't do that. I really am. I know you were embarrassed at the meeting, and frankly so was I.

Marvin: Good, I'm glad you are taking responsibility.

Andre: I think we should talk about how we prepare for client meetings in general. Because I honestly thought that you would have found out what the client wanted to discuss when you spoke with her.

Marvin: Are you putting the blame on me?

Andre: No, I'm not. I'm just saying we need to get on the same page on how we prepare.

Marvin: Okay.

Andre: I want to avoid this happening again, and so we need to clarify who has ultimate responsibility for things like this. I thought you had checked with the client, and you thought I had. So I think we need to coordinate and communicate better.

Marvin: I agree.

In this conversation, Marvin began the same way as he had in the first conversation. He immediately blamed Andre for "screwing up the meeting." The shift started with Andre's response. Rather than becoming defensive, Andre expressed regret about what happened as well as empathy for Marvin and his frustration. As a result, Marvin calmed down, and Andre was able to share his own emotions and frustration with how the meeting went. Andre even succeeded in getting Marvin to hear him out. Marvin also seemed open to discussing what happened and how this type of mistake could be prevented in the future. As a consequence of Andre's unilateral change in his response to Marvin, the overall dynamic changed, resulting in better behavior from Marvin.

WHAT ABOUT EXTREME PEOPLE?

I imagine that for many readers, doubts persist as to whether this advice would work in real life. You might be thinking, "Okay, I believe that a different response can change how the other person behaves in most cases. However, *my* case is different. My counterpart (boss, colleague, client, or subordinate) is truly extreme, and nothing will work in my situation."

This way of thinking divides the world into two types of people. There are the "normal" people, with whom we may disagree, argue, not get along, struggle, or fight, but who are rational and can be influenced by our own behavior. Then there are the "extreme" people, with whom nothing can work or will work, because they are crazy, evil, or stupid. There is no point is trying to fix or even improve things with the extreme people, because it's hopeless.

It is true that there are extreme people in the world who can't be reasoned with and can't be influenced. Indeed, my thinking on this topic was influenced by my sister, a psychother-apist who many years ago worked at an outpatient clinic for mental illness. She saw all types of people from many different professions, socioeconomic levels, and walks of life. And I'll never forget her advice to me during this time: "Donny," she said, "the mentally ill walk among us. It's the person behind you in line at the grocery store, or in front of you at the ATM, or sitting next to you in the movie theater." She was making the point that there are crazy people out there, and they may look completely normal on the outside but still be completely nuts.

So, allow me to stipulate that there are crazy (and evil and stupid) people out there, with whom the situation truly is hope-less. But that population of extreme people is actually a tiny fraction of the people most of us deal and struggle with daily. There is, I believe, a much larger population of folks who seem to us to be those extreme people when we are stuck. That is, these people aren't really crazy, stupid, or evil; nevertheless, we think they are, since we get into repeated stuck situations with them. Being stuck means that we have not determined any way to elicit a better version of these people. There is almost cer-tainly a way to make it better, but we simply haven't found it yet. And until we do, it's hard to believe it can ever be different.

This is an essential distinction, because once I declare the other person to be crazy, it's over. I am resigned to staying stuck, like Wendy, and never even get to try everything I could to make things better. But is Kevin evil? Is Wendy's boss stupid? Is Marvin crazy? Or is each of these people capable of being influenced, if they are approached in a different way? I believe they can be influenced. But that is something we can only find out by trying, and trying requires first assuming that something can be done. Only by trying "everything" (or at least many things) can we fairly declare that "nothing works."

It's a bit like doing a crossword puzzle. You struggle to find a word that will fit in the space you have, and even though it's hard, you keep trying, knowing that a solution does indeed exist. And if you don't keep trying, you won't find the answer.

But now imagine you were struggling with a particularly difficult crossword puzzle, and I told you that it's possible there is no solution. Suppose I told you that the newspaper occasionally publishes a crossword puzzle for which there is no solution, and it's impossible to tell in advance if this is one of those unsolvable ones. How hard would you try to solve it before you gave up, on the assumption that it was hopeless? (Thank heavens they don't make crosswords like that—imagine the frustration and suffering it would cause!)

The problem with stuck situations is analogous. They are puzzles to be solved, but because we all know that some situations cannot be fixed, our efforts at changing the dynamics that are changeable are undermined. We doubt change is possible, and we, like Wendy, prematurely throw up our hands in defeat. This book is all about fighting that temptation to give up.

I also want to clarify that I am not saying you need to change the personality of your counterpart in a stuck situation. In fact, chances are excellent that you can't change the other person. And you don't need to; all you need to do is to shift the other person's *pattern of interaction with you* just enough to get unstuck. Marvin may be the type of person who gets angry easily and yells. And maybe, even probably, he will always be that type of person. But if Andre handles his interactions with Marvin differently, he can nevertheless find a way to negotiate and collaborate more effectively with Marvin.

Still not convinced? Ask yourself this: Have you ever had a relationship or dynamic with someone where things were difficult, but then once you understood how to interact with that person, it got much better? If so, then you have had an experience where changing yourself changed the other person's behavior. And I'm willing to bet that before you found the key to changing that dynamic, you would have believed that the situation was hopeless and that this other person was resistant to change.

CHANGE WHAT YOU SAY

Consider the case of Brian, an analyst who worked in a consulting firm. As a senior manager he reported to Alice, the head of his practice area. In addition to working with clients, Brian and one of his peers, Jacob, managed a team of junior analysts. Brian and Jacob were jointly responsible for assigning the junior staff to various research projects, making sure employees were neither overworked nor underworked.

Tensions had arisen between Brian and Jacob as they tried to co-manage the junior staff. Brian wanted to be a team player and would regularly consult with Jacob over staffing decisions. Jacob, however, rarely checked in with Brian and would frequently act unilaterally, assigning work without ever consulting him.

Brian was frustrated that Jacob wasn't working collaboratively. He tried to share his frustrations with Jacob:

Brian: Jacob, I want to talk to you about the junior analyst team.

Jacob: Okay, what's up?

Brian: I think we need to get on the same page regarding staff assignments.

Jacob: Why, what's the problem?

Brian: I just think we should be aligned and coordinate what each of us is doing.

Jacob: That's fine. But things get really busy, and I need to assign people quickly.

Brian: Of course, everyone is busy. But we need to get in sync about staffing for the good of the team.

Jacob: Look, I just don't have time to meet with you to discuss assignments all the time. It's not personal; it's just not a high priority, given all the client-facing work and everything else that needs to get done.

Brian was upset by Jacob's comments, believing that Jacob was being disrespectful of his status as a peer and insensitive to his feelings. Brian felt stuck and didn't know what to do. As you now know, the first step is for Brian to recognize that he can change his dynamic with Jacob without convincing Jacob that Jacob has to change; Brian has the ability to shift his stuck situation with Jacob by being different himself.

But how, exactly, could Brian change this stuck dynamic? What could Brian say that would shift things with Jacob in a positive manner? Brian has many choices for how to proceed. Let me offer three examples that are meant to be illustrative, rather than an exhaustive list of responses.

One option would be for Brian to *express empathy* for Jacob's point of view. Demonstrating understanding and sensitivity to another person's situation and feelings is powerful. When you make another person feel heard, you set the stage for the other person to hear you. Empathizing is almost always helpful in a stuck situation, and learning to communicate empathy is a skill worth developing. To do that, Brian might continue the dialogue as follows:

Brian: It sounds like you feel that consulting and coordinating take a lot of time. And given all of your responsibilities, you don't have a lot of time to spare right now.

Jacob: That's right. While managing the junior staff is important, making sure the client-facing work is done right is more important. I don't want to sacrifice the work I do for clients by investing too much time in this staffing area.

Brian: I completely understand that. And I want to make sure that we come up with a way of coordinating staffing that is not overly burdensome to you.

Jacob: Good.

Brian: But I do have some concerns about how things are going now, and some ideas for what to do differently. Can I share those?

Jacob: Sure.

Here Brian has shown openness to Jacob's point of view and demonstrated that he takes Jacob's concerns seriously. This helps Jacob, in turn, become open to hearing Brian's point of view. By Brian changing his response to Jacob, Jacob will respond differently to Brian.

A second option would be for Brian to *show vulnerability and express his own feelings.* Many stuck situations become intractable because neither side wants to share emotions for fear of appearing weak. This can lead to a standoff, with no progress being made. Sometimes expressing one's emotions in a non-threatening and vulnerable manner can elicit empathy from the other side, changing the entire dynamic. In the original dialogue, Brian said he wanted things to change, but he did not share with Jacob how much Jacob's choices were bothering him. In the absence of Brian disclosing that he feels disrespected and upset, it is highly possible, and even likely, that Jacob doesn't realize that Brian's feelings were hurt. If Brian wanted to be more explicit about that, he might initiate a different dialogue, as follows:

Brian: Jacob, I understand that you don't want to spend more time coordinating. But when you make unilateral decisions and act without consultation, I feel you are not treating me like a peer or an equal.

Jacob: That's not what I'm trying to do.

Brian: Well, I need you to understand that, as co-managers of the team, we have to find a way to collaborate. And when you brush off the topic, I experience it as disrespectful, and frankly, it bothers me.

Jacob: Gee, I'm sorry about that.

Brian: So, let's try to find some middle ground.

Yet a third possibility would be for Brian to *be specific and concrete* with Jacob. It's easy to become bogged down in a theoretical argument about the relative merits of collaboration versus autonomy. Moving the conversation from something abstract to something concrete can catalyze a positive shift toward problem solving.

In the original conversation (described previously), Brian did not articulate what exactly he means by "getting in sync." If he were to discuss a specific option with Jacob, he might get a different response:

Brian: Let's find a way to balance your desire to be efficient and save time with my desire to coordinate and make sure we are balancing the load among the junior staff.

Jacob: I just don't want to spend a lot of time discussing staffing.

Brian: Here is my proposal—let's have a meeting once a week to go over staffing and to plan for the coming week. I don't think that meeting should take more than thirty minutes, and it will help me feel much more comfortable that we are working as a team. What do you think?

Jacob: I think I can spare thirty minutes per week.

Communicating with more empathy, expressing one's feelings clearly, offering a concrete plan for what to do—these are all unilateral changes that Brian can make to shift the dialogue and, by extension, the overall situation. Moreover, the different options don't have to be chosen separately; it's possible to use a combination of them in the same conversation. Brian can share his feelings and offer a more concrete option for discussing staffing. He can empathize with Jacob as well as share his own feelings. And it's crucial to remember that I am not saying this situation is Brian's fault and that Jacob is off the hook; Jacob could have handled things more skillfully himself by inquiring about Brian's feelings or showing sensitivity to Brian's concerns. These are simply ideas for what Brian could do differently to facilitate a different conversation. That alone can help him get unstuck.

CHANGE HOW YOU SAY IT

There are times when you can elicit important changes in your counterpart's response not by changing what you say, but simply altering how you say it. The impact of the technique you use for communication—the volume of your voice, how quickly you speak, whether you pause before responding, whether you inter-rupt—is tremendous. Changing these cues can alter your dynamic dramatically.

Consider once again the Andre/Marvin example. In the original conversation, things went poorly. And in the second version of their exchange, Andre was explicit in showing empathy to Marvin, which made a big difference. Another way for Andre to have elicited a shift in Marvin's behavior would have been to say the same thing he had said in the first conversation, but to use a different tone. Here is that same dialogue—only now, as you read it, pay attention to how Andre uses volume, speed, and pauses to alter the conversation:

Marvin (yelling): I can't believe that you screwed up that client meeting.

Andre (*pausing, then speaking in normal tone*): It wasn't my fault.

Marvin (*yelling*): Yes it was. Stop trying to pass the buck.

Andre (*softly and slowly taking a breath*): I don't appreciate you blaming me for your own mistakes. You were the one who scheduled the meeting, and I assumed you found out what the client wanted to discuss.

Marvin (*no longer yelling*): Well, I was relying on you to find that out since you were preparing the materials.

In the original conversation, where Andre did not alter his technique, Marvin responded by saying, "It's your job to prepare materials before a client meeting." In this instance, however, it's harder for Marvin to keep being so aggressive when Andre is changing the tenor of the conversation. Andre is deliberately removing energy from the system by lowering his voice, speaking softly, and breathing deeply. It's easy to yell at someone who is yelling back. It's harder to yell when the person you are yelling at is speaking even more softly than usual.

Andre's actions force Marvin to realize he was behaving in an unconstructive manner. Whereas in the first take, their conversation was more like a Ping-Pong match, where each player hits the ball harder and harder, ratcheting up the intensity with each retort, the change in tone makes the second take of the conversation a very different interaction, even though the words are the same.

When you find yourself stuck, my advice would be to consider changing not just what you are saying, but how you are saying it. In the context of how you are interacting, here are some variables to pay attention to:

> *Pace.* Should the pace of the dialogue be quickened or slowed?

> *Volume.* How loudly are you speaking? Should you raise or lower the volume of your voice?

> *Interruptions.* Are you interrupting other people, or are they interrupting you?

> *Pauses.* Can you wait and let the silence hang before answering the other person?

If you tend to speak quickly, try slowing down. If you tend to raise your voice, lower it. Or, alternatively, if you tend to lower your voice and respond meekly, increase your volume and respond more assertively. Pausing between when your counterpart says something and when you begin speaking is an effective yet underused means of changing an unconstructive conversation. Try allowing a brief silence to hang before you start talking, and notice the effect.

Some of these changes may be difficult to execute: If your natural tendency is to raise your voice when you are emotional, for example, it will take some self-control to do the opposite. And it may feel "unnatural" to do so. But keep in mind that the goal is to change things by changing yourself. If you keep doing the same thing you've been doing, things will probably continue as they have been. So try something new. And you don't need to make a dramatic shift. Even a small shift in your communication pattern can change the whole dynamic.

BEYOND THE CONVERSATION

Changing the dynamic to get unstuck is not limited to changing what you say or even how you say it. Sometimes the way to get unstuck is to *do* something different, to change the course of action, rather than to say something different. Let's look again at Brian's situation as an example; Brian has a range of options for what he might do.

One way of shifting things is to change the players. To unlock his stuck situation, Brian can find a different person to talk to: He can opt to approach his manager, Alice, and ask for her input and guidance, instead of talking to Jacob directly. Learning of Brian's concerns about staffing and the potential that it has to negatively impact the junior team, Alice might take the initiative to offer her own guidelines for assigning work and managing the team, which would inevitably shift the dynamic between Brian and Jacob. This strategy could be deployed before, after, together with, or in lieu of a direct conversation with Jacob.

A second possibility that might shift things would be for Brian to create an explicit structure to govern the staffing process. Such a structure could include, for example, a written set of staffing guidelines, an online spreadsheet for tracking staffing assignments, and/or a standing weekly meeting between Brian and Jacob, in which they review how junior staff is allocated. Creating this structure might itself shift the dynamic, since it would help solve Brian's concerns without making Jacob feel overwhelmed. Of course, for this solution to be optimal, Jacob would have to agree to the structure; even so, Brian's unilateral action would certainly push the issue forward, helping Brian to get unstuck.

A third option would be for Brian to change his own behavior regarding staffing. When a new project begins, he could review the available staff members and simply assign people himself, without consulting with Jacob as he had in the past. Brian might discover that indeed, it is more efficient to do some things without consultation, and that he could minimize the time and energy he was spending coordinating with Jacob. Alternatively, Brian's unilateral change might create discomfort for Jacob, making him aware of the problems caused by the lack of mutual consultation. Moreover, simply creating balance with his co-manager (i.e., creating a situation where each of them can act on his own) might reduce Brian's resentment and frustration toward Jacob. Either way, a change in Brian's behavior has significant potential to change the stuck situation.

Fourth, Brian could make an internal change by reflecting on his feelings. He might examine his own reaction by asking himself questions, such as: Why is this bothering me? Do I feel Jacob's behavior is harming the business, or is it just upsetting me? Could I reframe this situation so that I don't take it so personally? As we will see in Chapter Five, dispassionately and honestly examining one's own reactions and behavior can also open the door to shifting a stuck situation, without even engaging the other side.

Finally, there is always the option of leaving the situation. If all else fails, Brian can seek to transfer to another role within the company, or even look for a new job. This is, in some ways, like giving up. But it is nevertheless useful to keep in mind that leaving the situation is an option, because doing so is an additional way to fight one's hopelessness and resistance to trying to make things better.

As you struggle in your own stuck situation, try to remember that by doing things differently, you *create options* for yourself. Here are some questions to help you generate options for freeing yourself from your stuck situation:

- Could I change the conversation by changing the manner in which I communicate?

- Could I change the conversation by changing what I say? Can I effect change by expressing empathy toward the other person? By sharing my own feelings? By suggesting a concrete solution?

- Could I change the situation by speaking with someone else?

- Could I change things through action, by doing something different, instead of through talking?

- Could I change things by reflecting on my own feelings and making an internal shift?

- Could I change things by leaving the situation?

If being stuck feels like you are trapped in a maze with no way out, recognizing that you have options is like suddenly being shown that the maze has five doors that you can open. There is no way of knowing which door will lead to the way out, but recognizing that you have options can ignite the spirit to change and the will to try.

SUMMARY

When you are feeling hopeless, when you think nothing will make something better, you know you're stuck. That feeling leads people to give up. Overcoming hopelessness and becoming motivated to try something different is fundamental to getting unstuck. It is true that not every situation can be fixed. By suspending your own disbelief and by being optimistic, you have the opportunity to find out whether things can change. Assume for a moment that your situation might be fixable, and you will likely muster the will to try to make it different.

Taking the steps to make things different does not mean it is all your fault. The predicament isn't about *fault,* it's about *change.* We each have the ability to change any dynamic we're in, just by modulating our own behavior. Remember, discovering that you can change things by behaving differently yourself is wonderful news. It means that no matter who you are dealing with, or how difficult it is to talk to that person, you, on your own, have the power to adjust the dynamic.

There is a saying commonly attributed to Lao-tzu, the Chinese founder of Taoism: "A journey of a thousand miles begins with a single step." The move from standing still—feeling stuck—to taking that first step—changing yourself—is the all-important beginning on which the rest of this book is based.

But this chapter is only setting the stage for change. In the next chapter I will begin to share with you the "secret sauce" for how you can interact differently, which opens up whole new worlds of possibility, even in your most stuck situations.

CHAPTER 2

Shifting Perspective

Kent was a brilliant attorney at a major law firm. His percentage of cases won was among the highest in the state. His reputation as a top-notch litigator was one of the reasons clients chose Kent's firm to represent them.

Kent had a major weakness outside the courtroom, however; he was lousy at handling clients. Nervous litigants would meet with Kent before a major trial, seeking reassurance. Intensely focused on trial strategy, Kent would spend most of the meeting discussing the weaknesses in their case. Clients left more nervous than they were when they came in. Upon receiving this feedback, Kent said, "Look, the case does have weaknesses; I'm not going to hide that. Besides, if they don't trust me to handle the case, they shouldn't have hired our firm."

One of Kent's partners suggested that he try empathizing with his client's feelings. Attempting to apply this advice, Kent had the following exchange with a client:

Client: Kent, I'm nervous about this trial that's coming up.

Kent: Don't be nervous. What we need to do is to plan by focusing on the weaknesses of the case. There are several.

Client: I'm very anxious. A lot is riding on this case. I could lose my company over this lawsuit.

Kent: I hear what you are saying, but as I told you, the case has flaws. We made a decision not to settle, and I think it was the right one. Anyway, it's too late now. We need to talk trial tactics.

Client: I'm worried.

Kent: I'm empathetic to your feelings, but just forget about it. Worse comes to worst, we can appeal.

Client: Appeal? That could drag on for years!

Kent: Look, I'm trying to empathize. I know you feel nervous, but don't you trust me to handle your case? If we lose, we will appeal. We need to focus now.

Not surprisingly, this client did not feel good about this conversation. And Kent's reputation as being bad at handling client relationships did not improve either, harming the business. I'm sure you can relate to Kent's predicament. He wanted to improve in how he handled these difficult interactions, but he also felt strongly that clients needed him to be brutally honest. He was stuck.

Kent's partners suggested that he get coaching from an outside professional and enlisted my help to work with Kent on this issue. My initial conversation with Kent went as follows:

Me: What do you think the problem is?

Kent: Clients are extremely needy and are looking to me to make them feel better. I have tried to be empathetic, but really that is not my job.

Me: How would you define your job?

Kent: I'm their lawyer, not their therapist. My job is to win their case, not deal with their emotions. Besides, they shouldn't want me to be anything less than brutally honest.

Me: Why not?

Kent: Because if I am distracted by the need to make them feel better, they might not have the clearest possible picture of their case. When it comes to settlement offers, for example, they need to be empowered with facts in order to make hard choices. Litigation is inherently uncertain—they have to understand that.

Me: Is that what you would want from your lawyer?

Kent: Absolutely. I wouldn't want a therapist—I'll hire someone to give me psychological counseling if that's what I need. I want a cold, hard realist handling my legal case, someone who doesn't sugarcoat things.

Given Kent's mindset, it was not surprising that he was stuck, and that his attempts at showing empathy did not work. He could not understand what clients wanted from him. His experience was that when his partners asked him to show more empathy, they were in fact asking him to hide the flaws in clients' cases. He fundamentally could not grasp his clients' need for reassurance in the face of anxiety, and it showed in how he interacted with them.

Then, during one coaching session, Kent let me know that he might be interrupted with an important call. When the phone rang, it was clear that he had been awaiting the call anxiously. After listening to the caller, he said, "So what does that mean? No, I'm not asking for a guarantee, I just want to know what I am up against. . . . I realize you are the doctor, I'm just nervous here. Okay, bye." After hanging up, Kent said to me, "I can't believe this surgeon. I'm waiting for some test results, and I am consumed with worry. All I want to know is if I'll be okay. But he is totally indifferent to my feelings. He speaks to me in medical jargon that I don't understand and does nothing to reassure me. It may not be a big deal for him, but for me it's all I can think about. Doesn't he understand what I am going through? Why doesn't he get it?"

This was a golden opportunity to make a breakthrough, and I seized the moment:

Me: I think your doctor is just being honest with you.

Kent: Yeah, but it is freaking me out.

Me: Well, he's not your therapist; he's your doctor. His job is to be a realist and to honestly tell you the risks you are facing so that you can make choices about treatment.

Kent: Look, I see the parallel you are making to my interactions with clients. But it's not the same at all.

Me: Why not?

Kent: Because lawsuits are just about money. They are not that big a deal. We can always appeal. This is about health! That is far more important and far more anxiety-inducing than a lawsuit.

Me: I'm sure that's true—*for you*. But keep in mind that you have thirty years of experience as a lawyer. You've been involved in so many court cases that it's just not scary for you anymore. But for a client, it can be a frightening experience.

Kent: Maybe. But I might have to go in for *surgery*.

Me: Well, consider the surgeon's point of view. You are just one of many, many patients he has talked to and operated on in his career. Your medical issue is not necessarily that big a deal for him. So, of course, he is short and to the point. In fact, he might be getting coaching right now, and he might defend himself by saying the same things you have said to me in the past.

Kent: I see your point.

Me: I'm not justifying how your doctor is treating you. I'm simply saying that you and your doctor have vastly different perspectives on how to talk about your test results because you come from such different places. But the same holds true for you and your clients, only with the roles reversed.

Kent: I never looked at it like that.

Following this exchange with Kent, something shifted. Kent was able to show much more empathy toward his clients. While he was still a hard-nosed litigator, and while he insisted that clients review the weaknesses of the case with him, he was also able to soothe his client's fears somewhat, and at the very least show compassion for their feelings of anxiety.

So what changed for Kent? And what can we all learn from this example to help us get unstuck in our most difficult situations?

CHANGING YOUR THINKING

Sun Yat-sen, the famous Chinese statesman of the late nineteenth and early twentieth century, said: "To understand is hard. Once one understands, action is easy."[1] Changing how you communicate follows this same formula. The words you say and the actions you take are the outcome; the process of producing that outcome begins with your own thinking. And as Sun points out, mastering our own thinking and achieving understanding is hard. But that hard work is the only reliable path toward change.

What Kent experienced was a change in thinking, or a shift in his perspective. The word *perspective* comes from a Latin root, meaning "to look through." It is the lens through which you see the world. Just like a physical lens in a pair of glasses or a microscope, it shapes and filters what you see. It emphasizes some parts of the picture, bringing them into sharp focus, while other parts are deemphasized and blurred into the background. Your perspective is your point of view on an issue or situation. It is a function of many things—personality, experience, culture, and professional training, for instance.

How you see a situation matters a great deal, because it determines how you are able to respond to that situation. Your ability to make choices about how to react to your counterpart is a function of your thinking. Unless you change your thinking, you cannot truly change your course of action. The good news is that shifting perspective is something you can do unilaterally. And if you can change your thinking, a whole new world of possible skillful responses opens up for you.

Consider Kent and his perspective on client relationships. Kent saw his role as that of an expert with technical skills, hired to provide a specific service. His primary, perhaps only, duty was to deliver excellent legal service to his clients. Anything beyond that, such as dealing with clients' emotions, was not part of the job. Indeed, Kent felt that it might be risky for him to attend to those external factors, as they could distract him from focusing on the legal representation of the client. He didn't want his clients to be stuck in their feelings; he wanted them to be prepared and at their best for trial.

Kent's perspective is certainly reasonable. In many cases this is precisely what a client wants and needs. At the same time, Kent's perspective was preventing him from incorporating the feedback he had gotten from clients and from his partners. He was told that he needed to be more sympathetic to clients. But he simply could not appreciate why clients would want or need reassurance from their attorney. As a result, it was impossible for him to give that reassurance when all the while his mindset was telling him, "This empathy stuff is irrelevant and dangerous. Let me just get it over with, so I can go back to doing my job of litigating the case."

Contrast that with the perspective of Kent's partners. They felt that his job included providing his clients with legal advice and representation, as well as counseling and helping them navigate the difficult path through litigation. Kent's partners believed that the clients' feelings were fully within the scope of the service Kent should be providing as a counselor. While he must not let a client's emotions undermine his ability to represent them in litigation, he should wherever possible attend to those emotions, including showing compassion and empathy.

This second perspective is also reasonable and may reflect how many clients look at things (consciously or not) when they come to Kent with their anxieties. Once Kent was able to see this other perspective, his ability to interact more effectively with his clients was transformed. Suddenly, Kent was able to be more empathetic, instead of echoing phrases that didn't make his clients feel any better. Indeed, it was like turning a key in a lock, and everything shifted.

What opened Kent's eyes was having an experience similar to that of his clients. His own exchange with his surgeon—an expert he relied on but who failed to reassure him in the face of intense anxiety—radically reshaped his ability to understand his clients. Having found himself in a comparable situation, he was able to see their perspective. And that was what unlocked his ability to be different and change the overall dynamic.

It may seem difficult to believe that Kent could be so blind to his client's fears or needs, but it's quite common. One person does not understand—or sometimes even consider—where another person is coming from. We can all become imprisoned in our own points of view. But to truly be different, we need to break through the barriers and think differently. This book will show you different techniques for achieving your own mental breakthrough so that you, like Kent, can get unstuck.

DIFFERENT PERSPECTIVES CAN COEXIST

There is a joke about a couple who came to a rabbi to mediate their marital dispute. The rabbi invited the wife to speak first, and she spent several minutes explaining in great detail all of her husband's flaws and misdeeds. After she finished speaking, the rabbi paused, stroked his beard, and said, "You're right." The husband then protested, insisting that he be given a chance to share his point of view, which the rabbi invited him to do. The husband then took his turn to criticize his wife's behavior, as well as defend all the things he had done. After his diatribe, which lasted several minutes, the rabbi again paused and said, "You're right." At that point the rabbi's assistant, who had been listening and taking notes the whole time, jumped in and said, "Excuse me, rabbi, but first you listened to the wife and told her she was right. Then you listened to the husband and told him he was right. How can they both be right?" The rabbi again paused, turned to the assistant, and said, "You know what? You're right!"

We can use this humorous story to understand two important points. First, each of the quarreling spouses has a unique perspective, and within that perspective each of them is indeed right. Put another way, each one tells a story that makes sense, follows an internally consistent logic, and is valid. So, the rabbi can honestly tell the husband that he is right and the wife that she is right: Within their respective perspectives, given how they see things, what each of them said makes sense.

Second, the rabbi is also agreeing with the assistant, because while each spouse may have a story that makes sense in the individual's own mind, that does not mean both perspectives have to be equally "correct" in an objective sense. If the rabbi were being asked to judge between the husband and wife, rather than to mediate, he would not necessarily find both stories equally persuasive and simply split the difference. It's possible to both appreciate that there are multiple perspectives, each with its own internal logic, yet still maintain that one perspective is more objectively convincing than the other. And in that sense, the assistant is right as well.

This is a difficult concept: How can two opposing perspectives both be reasonable? The heart of the matter is that there is an essential difference between *seeing* another perspective and *agreeing* with another perspective.

Consider the following example: Nick was the managing partner for Acme Accounting. The firm had a number of departments corresponding to different practice areas, such as tax, audit, and consulting, each led by a department head. While the different department heads were responsible for their own departments, Nick was responsible for ensuring the continued growth and profitability of the firm as a whole.

Nick was having difficulties with Ted, the department head for tax. A thirty-five-year veteran in the industry, Ted was an acknowledged tax expert and an excellent manager. He had skillfully managed the division ever since taking it over twenty years ago, ensuring that clients received top-quality service and that junior staff members were mentored and cultivated for greater responsibility.

In recent years, however, the tax department had faltered, having lost a number of important clients. Nick's tension with Ted was over how to grow the department. Nick felt that the firm's corporate clients increasingly viewed tax services as a commodity, rather than a specialized area of expertise, and they were readily moving their business to a competitor to save money. Acme therefore needed to constantly be looking for new clients to replace the turnover. Nick wanted Ted to actively sell business to prospective new clients and to raise the firm's profile by speaking at conferences and engaging in other marketing activities.

Ted, on the other hand, felt that as the head of the tax department, his attention needed to be centered on serving existing clients and overseeing the work to make sure it was done perfectly. Focusing primarily on selling would undermine the firm's reputation for quality and excellent customer service, and it was contrary to how the firm had been successful in the first place.

Consider the following conversation between Ted and Nick:

Nick: Ted, you need to go out and sell more business.

Ted: That is not what I do, and it's not what we do at Acme.

Nick: And that is why you are losing so much business. What you are doing is not working.

Ted: What you want me to do will destroy us. I don't care if we lose half of our clients; cutting back on service and quality will ensure we lose the other half.

Nick: I know you don't like to sell, but the market is different than when you started out in your career. Wake up and smell the coffee—this is how accounting firms are run nowadays.

Ted: I am not a salesperson. People don't hire me as their accountant because I'm a good salesperson. They hire me because I am good at making sure their taxes are done right. You are asking me to change not just what I do, but who I am.

Nick: You are just being stubborn, and it's going to destroy the whole department.

Needless to say, things did not improve. Nick asked me to coach him on how to have a better conversation with Ted, so that he could persuade him to sell more business. Here is my coaching conversation with Nick:

Nick: Tell me what I can say that will change Ted's mind.

Me: Why do you think he is pushing back so hard?

Nick: I think he finds selling intimidating. And it's not something he enjoys doing. And he thinks we can succeed without it. But he is wrong. I have to show him that. How can I change his mind?

Me: Let's take a step back. Before we talk about what you can say, let's explore your perspective and Ted's perspective. Clearly, you feel that the industry has changed, and while at one time corporate clients would stick with the same accounting firm for many years, that is no longer the case. Clients will leave, and, as a result, firms such as yours need to go out and generate business to ensure growth or even to simply maintain your existing volume of business.

Nick: Correct.

Me: Now, let's look at Ted's view. What is he saying to you?

Nick: That he won't do it.

Me: Right. But why not?

Nick: Because he doesn't want to and doesn't like it. But he has to do it or his department will lose most of its clients.

Me: I think he may be saying more than just "I don't like selling." I think he is saying that he does not believe that clients will respond well to him becoming a salesperson.

Nick: Other firms are doing it successfully and taking a lot of market share from us. Selling is the most important function of senior partners, especially department heads.

Me: I'm not saying Ted is *right*. I'm saying you need to understand where he is coming from. In Ted's mind, you are asking him to be a different person.

Nick: I'm not.

Me: For him, these activities represent changing from "accountant" to "salesperson." Can you understand what a huge shift that is for him, and why he is fighting it?

Nick: I guess so.

Me: If someone pushed you to do something that violated your sense of who you were, you would fight it as well, wouldn't you?

Nick: Definitely. I sometimes have to fight back when clients push me to take a position that I am not comfortable with ethically.

Me: I think that is what he is doing here. And if you want to have a more effective conversation with Ted, you need to understand that that's how he sees your request.

Nick: Hmm. Well, that explains how stubborn he has been. But he is wrong about the industry, and his fears about clients are completely misguided.

Me: I'm not talking about who is right. I'm simply saying that if you just insist again and again that he is wrong, he will just keep fighting you. You need to address how he is looking at things.

Nick: I can try to do that.

Me: If you can talk about your different perspectives, and show him that you understand what his concerns are, you will be able to make progress.

The point of this coaching conversation was not to get Nick to agree with Ted. Rather, the goal was to help Nick see how Ted was seeing things. That does *not* mean Nick agrees with Ted; far from it. Indeed, it may very well be the case that Nick is absolutely correct on how the firm needs to respond to an evolving marketplace. But Nick was stuck in a battle with Ted. In order for Nick to speak more skillfully, he needed to see things through Ted's eyes.

Subsequently, Nick had a vastly different conversation with Ted:

Nick: Ted, I want to talk about how we can grow the department.

Ted: Okay. But you know I am not going to become a salesperson.

Nick: I've given it some thought, and I think all this time you've been pushing back because you feel I am asking you to change who you are.

Ted: You are right. I'm not about to change my career from tax department head to salesperson-in-chief.

Nick: I understand that. And if someone were pushing me to do something that I felt was not who I was, I would also resist, like you are.

Ted: Okay. I'm glad you can see that.

Nick: I am hoping we can find a way to integrate your feelings, about focusing on service rather than selling, with what I see as a change in the market.

Ted: What do you mean?

Nick: Well, there is no hiding the fact that we have lost a number of clients, and gained very few, in the last couple of years. I believe we are both committed to reversing that trend.

Ted: Definitely. That's why I want to provide top-notch work.

Nick: I agree. But our competitors, who have grown their tax departments at our expense, have done much more to market their services. I fear that if we don't do something similar, we could lose it all.

Ted: But why do I have to be the one to do that?

Nick: Maybe you don't. Maybe those tasks can be shared with someone else. Maybe there is a way for you to sell without your having to feel as if you're changing who you are. My point is, I now understand the source of your resistance, and I want to find a way to work with you, not just bend you to my plan.

Ted: That sounds good.

The more effective conversation between Nick and Ted was only possible once Nick could see Ted's point of view. He could then change the conversation with Ted and move the discussion forward from a win/lose battle to a shared challenge of finding a way to sell more business that would work for both Ted and the firm. But note: Nick was able to do this *without submitting or giving up his own point of view.* He still feels that more aggressive marketing is necessary, and he can continue to pursue that goal. But it starts with a better conversation with Ted. Nick was able to get unstuck—he thought differently, he had a different conversation, and now, he had new options to work with Ted in order to grow the business.

FLEXING YOUR MIND

What Kent and Nick (our two examples) and all of us need to learn is how to look at a situation from another point of view—not *instead* of our own perspective, but *alongside* our own perspective. We need to learn how to see multiple points of view at the same time. It's not a shift from "wrong thinking" to "right thinking." It's a shift from seeing only one subjective point of view to seeing multiple subjective points of view. That is the meta-skill for getting unstuck.

I refer to this meta-skill as acquiring a flexibility of mind. Your mind is like a muscle. The more you stretch a muscle, the more flexible and supple it becomes. You've probably seen yoga masters who, through years of practice, have achieved amazing levels of flexibility, allowing them to contort their bodies into all sorts of positions.

A flexible mind, then, is one that can stretch itself into many different mental positions with ease, each time looking at a situation from a different perspective. And the increase in mental flexibility comes from practice as well. The more you stretch your mind, the more agile and flexible it will be, with a cumulative effect over time. As you practice seeing other perspectives, your mind achieves greater flexibility and an increased capacity to see other points of view, even or especially those you disagree with.

NOW I SEE IT DIFFERENTLY

Cultivating the ability to see other perspectives can be transformative in various stuck situations. Sometimes, such as in Nick's case, shifting perspective helps you to have a more skillful conversation, although your view is the same as before you took in what the other side was thinking. In contrast, Kent was able to change and to become more empathetic to his clients, balancing this new attribute with his previous desire to dissect weaknesses in cases pretrial.

Sometimes a shift in perspective can dramatically alter a person's view of the situation. Louisa, an extremely bright senior manager at a large corporation, needed to reflect on the feedback she had received. She had again been denied a promotion to vice president, and when she asked why, her boss said, "Louisa, it has nothing to do with your technical expertise, your work ethic, or your commitment to the company. Everyone acknowledges how productive you are and how much you contribute to the business. It's simply a matter of your interpersonal skills. The people who report to you all say that you just don't listen to them. If you want to move ahead, you need to change that perception—people need to see you as someone they can talk to."

Being the ambitious person that she was, Louisa decided to hire a personal coach to help her get promoted. At their first meeting, Louisa explained the problem to the coach, describing her boss's feedback. At the end, Louisa said something revealing: "I want you to teach me how to look like I am listening," she told the coach.

"I beg your pardon?" the coach said. "Don't you mean you want to learn how to actually listen?" And Louisa answered: "God, no, I don't have time to listen to everyone's sob stories or silly ideas! I just need to learn the technique—body language, facial expressions, and so on—so that my subordinates will think I am listening to them, and I can get promoted."

We can all laugh at this story. Of course you can't teach people to look as if they are listening to someone else. People can spot a fake—maybe not right away, but over time Louisa's coworkers will realize that she is still not listening at all, but is simply better at pretending and deploying the trappings of listening.

Louisa's problem is that she is trying to change her behavior while leaving her perspective untouched. This doesn't work. In

Kent's initial attempt to be more empathetic to his clients, he said many of the common buzzwords and phrases people use to show sympathy, such as "I hear what you are saying" and "I empathize with you." But it didn't work for him, it won't work for Louisa, and it won't work for you, reader, unless you make the internal change first.

What is the best way for Louisa to appear as if she is listening? To actually listen! But for Louisa to *actually* listen, she would need to think differently about her interactions with her subordinates in general. Consider the following exchange I might have with Louisa:

Me: Louisa, why don't you try actually listening to your subordinates?

Louisa: I don't have time.

Me: What do you mean?

Louisa: They will come to me with a problem, and I know the solution. I will tell them the solution, but instead of thanking me, they get upset. They want to take fifteen minutes walking me through all of the details of the issue, sharing their deliberations, and so on. I have several people reporting to me who want to take up my time this way. I can't afford to waste that time. I am extremely busy and need to move on to other things.

Me: So saving time is the biggest issue for you?

Louisa: It's not just time. It's also the energy. It can be exhausting to listen to their whining. I'm solving their problem—doesn't that show that I care? Having long conversations about it is just not something I like to do.

Clearly, Louisa's perspective on her conversations with subordinates was getting in her way. She saw those conversations as purely technical. What was being transacted was the work that needs to be done. Her subordinates' need to share their deliberations and spend time discussing things with her was, in her mind, a distraction and a waste of time.

In order for Louisa to change, she needed to reframe her view of these conversations. Consider the following conversation:

Me: Louisa, I understand why you don't want to listen to your subordinates. It feels like a waste of time, and it drains your energy.

Louisa: Exactly.

Me: And I think that even if I taught you techniques to "look like you are listening," as long as you believed that conversations with your subordinates were a waste of time, it would show through. People would figure out that you weren't really listening.

Louisa: Well, I don't know what to do then. I want to get promoted, but I can't see wasting endless amounts of time to get there.

Me: Well, maybe you need to reframe, in your mind, what it means to spend time listening to your subordinates.

Louisa: How so?

Me: It may feel like a waste to you because you are only considering the concrete outcome of the conversation, which is solving their problem. Because you have the answer after one minute of conversation, the next fourteen minutes, which don't advance you to a different or better answer, are a waste.

Louisa: In most cases, that is exactly right. It feels like an enormous waste.

Me: But there is more to relating to subordinates than just getting to the right answer on a work question. You are overlooking the opportunity you have to improve your relationships or, conversely, the damage you are doing to these relationships with how you behave.

Louisa: What do you mean?

Me: When one of your staff members comes to you with a problem, there are actually two issues in play. One is the concrete problem that needs solving. The other is your relationship with that staff member. You seem to be good at solving problems but tend to ignore the whole issue of the relationship. When you cut people off, they feel ignored and devalued, and the relationship suffers. But if you spent more time talking to them and giving them your attention, you would not be "wasting" that time. You would be *investing* it in something other than the problem; you would be investing it in improving your relationship with that person.

Louisa: I see what you are saying. But following your advice would be quite unnatural for me. Once I see the answer, my natural instinct is to just blurt it out and move on. Continuing to talk feels strange. And it takes too much time, which I don't have.

Me: You don't need to engage in endless conversations. I understand that you cannot spend a full fifteen minutes, but perhaps you could take five minutes for these conversations. Also, if you saw the extra talking not as a "waste" but as an investment, it might feel less strange and less frustrating. We can work together on finding a style and rhythm for managing these interactions with subordinates, a way that feels right to you. But before we do that, I want to ask—are you on board? Does it feel like something worth investing in?

Louisa: I think so. I would like to have stronger relationships with my staff, and I can see how the things you suggest will help. Plus, this is what my boss is telling me I should be doing. So, let's give it a try. I do want that promotion.

Louisa's reflection on her situation allowed her to not only see a new perspective, but to adopt it as well. She came to understand that her conversations with subordinates were both about the work *and* about the relationship. Reframing things this way was a game-changer. Having achieved this mental breakthrough, the next step was to help Louisa balance listening attentively with keeping to a reasonable time investment for these conversations.

The change in mindset allowed Louisa to embrace her subordinates' desire for more conversation with her. This is one possible outcome from a shift in perspective. Contrast that with Nick, who remained convinced that his accounting firm needed to sell more business. He continued to disagree with department head Ted, but he was better able to address Ted's fears of being forced to become someone he was not. For Kent, the trial lawyer, the shift in perspective allowed him to feel true empathy for his clients, even while pushing them to make sober decisions about the litigation.

What all three of these examples have in common is that the change in the interaction was preceded by an internal shift in thinking. Each of them got unstuck by considering their respective counterpart's perspective. That is the foundational skill, the meta-skill, that will allow you to get unstuck in even your toughest situations.

WHAT'S THE MAGIC WORD?

When it comes to communication skills, most people want to focus on words—what to say and how to respond. As you can tell, that's not my philosophy. I believe that words are the output of the process, not the driver of it. But given how common the approach is, I want to take time to be explicit about why I see things as I do.

I had a client named Gail who asked me to teach a workshop on communication skills to a group of newly promoted managers. Feeling that this group struggled with delivering tough messages, she framed her request for a practical workshop as follows: "Can you give them a list of the three best opening lines for beginning a tough conversation? I'd also like the group to walk away with tips for how to share negative feedback. Maybe we could have a 'top-ten list' for how to say no, or 'five best practices' for delivering a difficult message."

While Gail's request for a "top-ten list" was a bit extreme, her desire for concrete advice was not. Like many managers, Gail was asking for a "communication formula," a recipe of skillful words and phrases to use in tough situations. I have three objections to formulas:

1. *No formula will work in all situations.* Imagine that I need to succinctly and directly tell my coworkers that I am taking vacation at the end of the month. If I am informing one of my subordinates, I might say, "I'm planning on taking vacation at the end of the month for a family wedding. Here are the things I will need you to do while I am out. Let me know if you have any questions." If I am informing my boss of my intentions, I might say, "I have a family wedding at the end of the month and would like to take vacation. I have a plan to cover my responsibilities while I am out, and I wanted to let you know this was my intention and to see if you have any questions or concerns." While the messages are both succinct and direct, the words and the tone are adapted to the different audiences. Using the more forceful tone with my boss is likely to antagonize her. Using the deferential tone with my subordinate is likely to undermine my own authority.

Thus, difficult situations are infinitely varied; the "right" words that someone learns to use in one context can be the wrong words in another. Variables such as hierarchy, the nature of the relationship (personal vs. professional), and the personality of the person you are speaking with all impact the choice of what to say. Choosing the right words will always need to be adapted to the context.

2. *A formula does not take into account the individual personality, style, and culture of the person applying it.* I am always surprised by books that provide specific words to say without recognizing that those words won't suit all readers. Unlike "one size fits all" gloves that are made of a stretchy material to expand

to perfectly fit the wearer's hand, whatever size it may be, I don't know of any phrases or sentences that are similarly universally fitting to everyone. People need to adapt communication strategies that allow them to be true to themselves and their style.

3. *Communication formulas are a distraction from the hard work of making real changes.* These words can end up becoming worse than worthless, as people hide behind a catchphrase and use it as an excuse to claim they are being different, when nothing at all has changed. That won't get you unstuck. If anything, trying to say what you think are the right words without changing your thinking will get you more stuck—you'll feel as if you are trying everything, but the situation at hand won't really be different.

SHIFTING PERSPECTIVE AND WRITING YOUR OWN MAGIC WORDS

Learning a phrase or a magic word is the cotton candy of communication skills—it's light, easy, and fun, but ultimately insubstantial. Shifting perspective, in contrast, is like eating your spinach—it's harder to do and takes discipline, but it will lead to long-lasting benefit.

Not only is shifting perspective a prerequisite for truly changing how you communicate, but it will allow you to come up with your own skillful responses to any challenging situation you face. A metaphor that comes to mind is cooking. A great chef knows how to cook delicious, healthy, and nutritious food. Anyone can taste the food and acknowledge how skilled the chef is. But how does one become a master chef? A cousin of mine studied culinary arts and explained to me that cooking school isn't about learning recipes. It's about mastering the underlying skills, such as cutting, braising, roasting, and sautéing. Once a chef has mastered those underlying skills, creating delicious food by following one recipe or another is simple. The recipes are the last and least important part of learning to be a superb chef.

In a similar fashion, the challenge in communication is *not* finding the right words—the right "recipe." Of course, words matter; they are what our interlocutor hears when we speak. But making a list of the right words to say and the wrong words to avoid isn't the way to go. Great cooks not only can follow any recipe, they can *devise their own recipes,* depending on the situation (and depending on what is left in the refrigerator at the end of the week!). Great communicators don't focus on key phrases. Rather, before they even open their mouths to speak, they have applied profoundly important foundational skills that allow them to succeed. In this book, I want to help you master those underlying skills for great communication. Once you've done that, coming up with the right words on your own will be easy.

The underlying skill for a chef involves cooking technique. The underlying skill for being different in a stuck situation is shifting perspective. If you can master that, you will be able to create your own "magic words" each time, customized to fit whatever audience and context you encounter.

SUMMARY

In this chapter we have located the challenge in getting unstuck to be primarily in our minds. To communicate differently is to think differently. Formulas and catchphrases don't work.

What does work is acquiring the ability to see your stuck situation from another point of view. This shift in perspective will unlock your ability to communicate differently. I refer to this skill as the ability to flex one's mind. Achieving a flexible mind is the goal, and it requires sincerely opening oneself up to seeing other points of view. You need to eat your spinach.

Later chapters of this book will present specific techniques to help you flex your mind. But first, we need to examine in greater depth why flexing one's mind can be so difficult, as well as the complex defense mechanisms people use to avoid doing it.

CHAPTER 3

Overcome Your Own Defenses

TEARING DOWN THE WALLS

Alex was complaining to Holly, the human resources manager of his company, about his personal assistant. "It's been three months, and she still messes up my calendar. She doesn't know which meetings should get priority or how much time to allocate—she is constantly checking with me before scheduling anything, which defeats the whole purpose of having an assistant. It's driving me crazy!" Alex was meeting with Holly to request that she replace his assistant with someone new, someone competent to do the job.

Holly was reluctant to do that. Alex's current assistant, Annie, was the third he had worked with this year. His first two assistants did not work out, either; one quit after a month, the other was let go after three months. Moreover, Annie had excellent reviews from the people she had worked with before.

Holly asked Alex's coworkers, including his previous assistants, for their input, and the feedback told a different story. Alex was a difficult person to work with. He had specific and confusing rules about how his calendar should be organized and when meetings could be scheduled. For example, he wanted all client meetings scheduled between 10:00 a.m. and noon, except for senior clients, who could come between 9:00 a.m. and 11:00 a.m., but not on Tuesdays, unless there was an emergency. In addition, because Alex never took the time and energy to explain what was behind his system, or who was considered a senior client, it was hard to know how he wanted things done. When his assistants asked for guidance, he would say, "It's all intuitive—any intelligent person should be able to pick it up as they go along." The combination of his rigid and hard-to-predict preferences with his refusal to invest time in training anyone ensured that he was consistently unhappy with his assistants.

Holly felt certain that the problem was not with the quality of the staff, but with Alex. She tried to raise the issue with him, but he rejected it completely:

Holly: Alex, I think the quality of the assistants I am sending you is quite good.

Alex: No, it's not. These people don't understand how to do anything.

Holly: Maybe you need to spend more time training them on what you want.

Alex: I do spend time training them. But they want me to spoon-feed them. I don't have time to constantly answer questions about this or that scheduling conflict. If they can't take initiative and figure it out, then this isn't the job for them.

Holly: Look, this is the third person you've worked with this year. Do you really think they are all incompetent? Maybe part of the problem is your expectations.

Alex: I think you are not offering high enough starting salaries and not recruiting people that have the talent and skill needed to do this job well. Just because you send me three unsuitable people, all of whom I reject, that does not mean my standards are too high. The issue is the quality of the candidates.

Holly: So basically it's everyone else's fault, and there is nothing you can do differently to make things better?

Alex: I wouldn't put it that way exactly, but essentially, yes.

Alex was stuck in a cyclical dynamic where he couldn't work with any of his assistants. While it may seem obvious to us, as neutral outside observers, that Alex was the problem and that his demands were unreasonable, that's not how he saw it. Alex was actively *resisting* seeing his own role in the situation. He is, in his conversation with Holly from HR, failing miserably at taking any perspective other than his own.

If shifting perspective were easy, I wouldn't be writing this book. It's not easy—it is actually quite difficult. This chapter explores why, which then sets the stage for the practical techniques and strategies for overcoming these barriers as detailed in later chapters.

There is a joke about a football player who keeps making mistakes, messing up the plays, and confusing the other players. The coach becomes exasperated and finally asks the hapless player, "Are you ignorant or simply indifferent?" The player replies, "Coach, I don't know and I don't care."

The challenge to shifting perspective can be broken down into two general categories. The first relates to passive ignorance—people are not aware that they even have a perspective and that others might see things differently. The second relates to active indifference or resistance—we don't care that the other side may see things differently; we only want to see things our own way.

PERSPECTIVE IS PRACTICALLY INVISIBLE

I have compared perspective to a physical lens that allows you to see the world. It is through your mental lens—your perspective—that you interpret and make sense of what you experience.

But precisely because your perspective is the lens through which you view the world, it is very difficult to look at. It would be like using your camera to take a picture of your camera's lens—you would need to take apart the camera first to get at the lens, but then how could you take the picture? We look *through* our perspective; it's quite difficult to look *at* our perspective. This makes it difficult to recognize that our perspective is only one among many, such that we might seek out other points of view.

Consider the following scenario: Irene and Lisa are good friends who just graduated from college. Irene lives in Boston and Lisa in New York City. Although they are close, their personalities could not be more different. Irene is extremely social and outgoing, with lots of friends. She shares a large house with several roommates and enjoys communal living. She loves hosting guests and traveling to visit her friends. Socializing in a group is her preference—the more the merrier!

Lisa, on the other hand, is a classic introvert. She lives in a studio apartment in Manhattan and cherishes the privacy and quiet it affords her. She also enjoys spending time with friends, but prefers to do so one-on-one, rather than in large groups. She is extremely loyal to those close friends and tries to always be there for them.

Irene and Lisa also have different communication styles. Irene is blunt and direct, while Lisa tends to be more circumspect.

Now consider the following conversation between these women:

Irene: Hi, Lisa, how's it going?

Lisa: Great. How are you?

Irene: I'm good. Listen, my sorority is having a big party for alumni in New York City next week, and I am planning to come to the city.

Is it okay if I stay with you for the weekend? I thought it would be a good chance for us to hang out.

Lisa: Hmm. (*Pauses.*) Normally I'd love to; I just don't know if I can do it this weekend. I guess I might be able to move things around, if it's really the best weekend for you, but I'm just not sure. I'll have to check.

Irene: Okay, great. Thanks.

Because of their different personalities and styles, Irene and Lisa bring different perspectives to this conversation. Their lenses for understanding it are radically different, and as a result, Irene and Lisa draw almost opposite conclusions on what was communicated in this exchange.

Irene believes that Lisa would be happy to have her over and simply needs to find out if it's possible. This is in line with Irene's general perspective on the world, as a social, extroverted type of person. In support of her view, she can quote the fact that Lisa said specific things such as, "I'd love to," and "I might be able to move things around." Given where Irene is coming from, that conclusion makes perfect sense.

Lisa, in contrast, feels she was tactfully but clearly signaling to Irene that it's not a good weekend for her. This is consistent with her general personality as an introverted, reflective person who doesn't like to confront others. In support of her view, she can point to the fact that she hesitated before answering, remarking, "I just don't know," "I guess I might be able to," and "I'm just not sure." Given Lisa's personality and style, her conclusion also makes perfect sense.

The perspectives of these two friends are miles apart. For Lisa, having Irene over is an imposition; for Irene, coming for the weekend is no big deal. Because they start out seeing the situation in different ways, they each hear the conversation differently. And each one can justify why she sees the conversation as she does.

Ask yourself—which of these characters do you identify with? Do you feel Irene should have been sensitive to Lisa's subtle cues signaling that it's not a good weekend? Or do you feel that Lisa should have expressed her feelings more explicitly, since she can't possibly expect Irene to read her mind? Your personality, culture, and communication style all shape the perspective through which you read this dialogue and, by extension, the conclusions you ultimately draw about it. Your view on this short conversation says as much about you as it does about the dialogue itself.

What is so tricky about perspective is that it sits in the background. As Irene is having this conversation, she is not saying to herself, "Well, I am a very direct and extroverted type of person, which colors how I hear what Lisa is saying." Nor is Lisa likely to think, "I tend to be indirect, so maybe my message was completely missed." Each person is simply interacting in this situation in the manner that makes sense to her.

What happens when these two friends try to clarify things? The problem does not go away easily. Imagine that Irene initiated a follow-up conversation about the weekend, just to make sure she and Lisa were on the same page:

Irene: I'm following up on our earlier conversation. I'd really like to come this weekend, but not if it will create a problem. Have you checked if this weekend will work for you?

Lisa: I haven't really checked.

Irene: Well, what do you think?

Lisa (*sighing*): I guess it is okay.

Irene: Great.

Irene walks away from this conversation thinking, "I'm glad this worked out." Lisa walks away from this conversation thinking, "She is so pushy. Can't she take a hint? I can't *believe* she is coming after all that."

Even after the follow-up conversation, the gap in their understanding remains. It's unfortunate, but it makes sense that this would be the case. We can understand why if we explore each side's perspective more deeply. Consider the following exchange I might have with Irene:

Me: How do you feel about your conversation with Lisa?

Irene: I feel good. I'm glad this weekend is going to work out.

Me: Do you think she has any hesitations about it?

Irene: Nah. I know she needs to be pushed to be more social sometimes, which I don't mind doing. I am usually the one initiating our visits, but once we get together it's always great.

Me: She sounded as if she wasn't really sure.

Irene: Well, only at the beginning. That's why I specifically said to her that I would not come if it was a problem. I explicitly invited her to share her feelings, and it would have been fine for her to say no. I even called to follow up and make sure it still worked. She could have spoken up then, but she didn't. That means it is fine. Trust me, it's happened before.

Me: But maybe she is uncomfortable being direct?

Irene: Look, we are close friends. She knows she can be honest with me. She said she will make it work, so obviously it's not a big deal. I think you are reading too much into what Lisa said.

Not only does Irene miss that she and Lisa are not on the same page, when it is suggested that Lisa may have a different perspective, Irene defends her own point of view and doesn't even know what I'm talking about. Irene explains why she is not misreading things, instead insisting that I am "reading too much into what Lisa said." This is not because Irene doesn't want to be open-minded. She just can't see beyond her own perspective.

Indeed, she can't even imagine that Lisa would not just say exactly what was on her mind.

Lisa suffers from the same problem, only in reverse. Consider the following conversation with Lisa:

Me: How do you feel about your conversation with Irene?

Lisa: Frankly, I'm frustrated.

Me: Why?

Lisa: Because Irene can be so pushy. I love her dearly, but she just won't take no for an answer.

Me: What do you mean?

Lisa: I basically told her not to come, but she kept pushing the issue.

Me: Do you think you were clear with her?

Lisa: Absolutely.

Me: Why didn't you just say, "Look, it's not a good weekend?"

Lisa: Well, I think I was clear that it wasn't optimal for me. And anyway, if she is pushing that hard, it must be very important to her, so I will find a way to make it work. I'm not going to just say "no way" to my friend.

Me: But maybe she would have preferred that you be blunt and clear.

Lisa: Bluntness isn't my style. Besides, I don't think you are reading this right. Irene *really* needs to come this weekend, so I will make it work somehow.

Attempts at improving the communication crash into the brick wall of Lisa's perspective. She can't see that her version of "direct" is unclear to Irene, and she struggles to see that Irene would have welcomed, even preferred, a more explicit discussion of Lisa's feelings about the visit. In fact, Lisa thinks she is being accommodating, and she sees Irene's directness as indicative of "really needing" something—because, after all, Lisa herself, with her indirect style, would have pushed as "hard" only if she absolutely needed to.

Why didn't the clarifying conversation clarify things? Because the conversation between these two friends was limited to the narrow issue of whether Irene could come visit for the weekend. The larger issue of their different socializing preferences was never discussed. Moreover, each of them participated in the conversation from behind the barrier of her perspective. What they each said and what they each heard was all filtered through their own lens. The difference in their communication styles—Irene's directness compared with Lisa's subtlety—was never addressed or even noticed.

Let's imagine that this pattern recurred over time, and that Lisa often hosted Irene when she didn't want to. She then reacted with veiled hostility, such that Irene didn't understand why Lisa was so unpleasant. It's easy to see how repeated wear and tear of this sort could fray their strong friendship. How could these two well-intentioned friends overcome their differences and have a meeting of the minds about the weekend? As noted in Chapter One, only one of them has to change to make things different.

First, they would need to consider the fact that the words they were using were not understood in the same way. They would need to flex their minds and consider that a difference in perspective was causing them to misunderstand each other.

Once the macro issue of perspective becomes part of their conscious thinking, the next step is to discuss the issue explicitly. Their dialogue can be transformed if they talk from outside their perspectives and have a discussion that recognizes and bridges their differences.

Such a shift in the conversation could be initiated by either one of them. For Lisa, it might involve saying, "It's not a good weekend for me, but it's hard for me to say that, because I don't want to reject you or let you down. But I'm trying to be honest and direct, which is not my natural style. How important is this weekend to you? Can we find another week that works better?" Alternatively, Irene could say, "Lisa, I hear some hesitation in your voice, and even though I am inviting you to say no, perhaps you don't want to hurt my feelings. I can be pushy and sometimes run people over, and I don't want to do that. What do you really think about the weekend? I truly want you to be honest with me; you won't be letting me down if you do that." Doing so would move the conversation from talking *through* their respective lenses to talking *about* their respective lenses.

By acknowledging their perspectives, Lisa and Irene can generate more options for navigating the weekend. Instead of Lisa feeling terrible about saying no, or suffering through the weekend, she could be honest about hosting being inconvenient for her. She and Irene could then decide together about what was best—and perhaps they could tweak the arrangement such that Irene could stay over, but in a way that was amenable to Lisa. Similarly, Irene wouldn't have to refrain from asking altogether, or alternatively suffer through Lisa being unkind to her for what seemed like no good reason. Irene could decide whether it was worth asking Lisa to put her up at all, or if she could find another friend to host her and spend time with Lisa without staying in her apartment. Pushing the conversation to the macro level would facilitate an honest dialogue about what got these friends stuck and allow them to talk about their different perspectives on what would be a good plan. They would probably end up having a more enjoyable weekend as well.

FREEING YOURSELF FROM PERSPECTIVE IGNORANCE

Neither Lisa nor Irene is consciously trying to avoid seeing her friend's perspective. Irene and Lisa are simply unaware of how their differences shape the dynamic between them. They are not willfully ignoring the role that their own personalities, preferences, and styles contribute to the difficulties they sometimes face in their relationship.

Seeing one's perspective—looking at the lens we look through—is hard. Part of what makes it hard is that our perspective doesn't feel like a perspective; it feels like objective reality. It's hard to get comfortable with the idea that our views on our stuck situations are actually subjective points of view. A tool called the Ladder of Inference, developed by Chris Argyris at Harvard Business School, can help clarify this distinction.[1] The Ladder of Inference describes how people think and make sense of their experiences. I'm using it here in a particular way: to help us as we grapple with the concept of objective reality vs. perspective.

Argyris's metaphorical ladder contains ascending rungs, each referring to a step in a person's thinking process. In my simplification of the original design, there are three rungs: data, interpretation, and conclusion.

The lowest rung, data, refers to all the information that one absorbs from the environment. The world is full of data. Everything you see, hear, read, and experience—all of it is information. In fact, there is far too much information out there for anyone to take it all in. So your brain does something important—it filters that information. Your brain filters *in* what is important and filters *out* whatever is deemed unimportant. Thus, the first rung of the ladder, data, is a small subset of all the data that actually exists in the world. It is only the data that makes it past your filter into your conscious awareness that can be used in your thinking.

For example, when I get onto a crowded subway car, I am bombarded by information—what people are wearing, what they are doing, who they are talking to. I can't possibly take it all in. Instead, my brain filters the information, in my case looking for two things: first, which people seem like they might be a little crazy and should be avoided, and second, where can I sit down. The rest of the available data is filtered out and doesn't even make it to my conscious thinking process.

The next rung of the ladder is interpretation. This is the process of thinking about the data that one has collected and deciding what it means. For example, while on the subway car, I see an empty seat next to a person who makes eye contact with me and smiles. The smile itself, which I notice, is a data point. But how do I interpret it? I might think the smile means that person is friendly. Or I might interpret a smile to a stranger on the subway as a sign that this person is a bit "off." As I try to decide which interpretation is more accurate, I may look for more data, such as what this person is wearing and doing. The process of gathering data and making interpretations repeats in a cyclical fashion.

The top rung of the ladder is one's conclusion, which is the outcome of all the intake of data and interpretation of that data, leading one to form an opinion or make a decision on whatever the topic is. In my example, my conclusion might be that it is safe to sit next to this person (or not).

The Ladder of Inference is a model that is quite intuitive. Indeed, upon reading this material, I expect you are thinking, "Yes, that all makes sense, but so what?" The "so what" is that Argyris's model highlights something crucially important: Although we may not experience it as such, there is *subjectivity* at every step of our thinking process.

Let's start with data. Data seems to be objective. Facts are facts, right? Right. But what matters is not what facts actually exist in the world, but what facts we pay attention to and remember. Those are the only facts that exist for us; the rest gets filtered out as noise and does not influence our thinking. And this model makes it clear that the data-gathering process is subjective and highly influenced by the motivations of the person conducting it. On the subway, I was scanning for a safe place to sit because that was what was important to me, and the data I absorbed reflected that concern. Nearly everything else was blocked out. But what if a police officer were to get on the subway car? She would likely be scanning for very different things, such as suspicious packages or potential pickpockets. As a result, her data set would look different from mine. What about an employee of the transit authority? He would likely be scanning for yet different data, such as whether the train was on time, how crowded it was, and how much litter was on the floor. Three people can be on the same subway car at the same time but notice very different data. This means they will have a different set of "facts" to think about, and they may develop different perspectives as a result.

The interpretation phase is highly subjective as well. This is where we apply our thinking to the data we noticed. You can think of the distinction between data and interpretation as the distinction between facts and meaning. Facts are objective and verifiable. If I had a video camera recording the subway car as I looked around, I could prove as a fact that the person with the empty seat next to him smiled at me. But facts are not the whole story, or even the most important part of the story. Deciding what a fact means is essential for functioning in the world. The analysis of facts to paint an overall picture, tell a story, make a decision—this is what people do every day, all the time, quickly and often subconsciously.

While on the train, I observe someone speaking in a loud voice. Does a raised voice mean the person is aggressive? Excited? Intoxicated? Hard of hearing? It's difficult to know for sure. Different people can interpret the same data point in vastly different ways. Many variables influence how people tend to interpret data. Culture is one example. In the United States, a raised voice means something quite different than it does in, say, southern Italy. Gender, age, personality—all of these variables influence how people interpret data.

Biases can also affect our interpretation of the data we take in. Social psychologists have documented many cognitive biases that influence how people gather and analyze information. One example is the confirmation bias in which people selectively gather, remember, and interpret data, doing so in a way that tends to confirm their existing beliefs.[2] Consider two senior executives, Pablo and Nancy, who are debating whether to promote an employee named Suzie. Pablo wants to promote Suzie, while Nancy does not think a promotion is warranted. The partners agree to delay the decision for one month and to spend the next thirty days observing Suzie's performance to see if a clearer picture of her worthiness for promotion will emerge. At the end of the month Pablo and Nancy meet again, and they are, each of them, even more convinced of their initial opinion of Suzie. Why? In the intervening month, Pablo took note of every time Suzie did something good, seeing further evidence that he was right. Nancy took note of every mistake Suzie made, seeing further evidence that she was right. Neither Pablo nor Nancy is deliberately seeking to shore up their respective position; it just tends to work that way. Even assuming both of them remember true facts, their data sets look so different because they had opposite biases as they gathered data. These biases in data collection are then magnified as both Pablo and Nancy interpret the data about Suzie to reconcile it with their own, preexisting opinions of her. Pablo maximizes every positive thing Suzie did and explains away or minimizes the negatives. Nancy does the reverse.

In this case, both Pablo's and Suzie's perspectives can be legitimate, because each of them has based the assessment of Suzie on objectively verifiable facts. If they then met to discuss whether Suzie would get promoted, they would probably get stuck. They'd each see their respective position as rooted in data and would be unaware that their data collection was itself shaped by their perspectives.

This same model can be applied to Lisa and Irene's situation. If, when asked about a weekend visit, a person tells her friend, "I'm not sure . . . I might be able to move things around; I just don't know if I can do it this weekend," is she making it clear that this is a not a good weekend? That sentence constitutes a data point, but Lisa and Irene interpret it in nearly opposite ways. For Lisa, the statement is tantamount to saying, "I'm sorry, but it's not a good weekend." For Irene, it means, "Maybe, let me check." The point is not who is right here. The point to make is that if either Lisa or Irene were made aware that the other person's perspective may be totally different, they could have a much more constructive conversation.

Just knowing about the Ladder of Inference can help all of us to pay attention to the subjectivity of our thinking. Recognition and awareness that each person's perspective is the product of a subjective process can make it easier to momentarily set aside one's own point of view and to look at the situation through someone else's eyes. It doesn't mean you have to give in, and it doesn't mean you concede that the other person is right and you are wrong. It just means that, in a world where we each have a subjective point of view, your flexible mind can look at things in more than one way. Flexing is temporary; you can revert back to your own point of view after you've flexed. But you must have the *ability* to flex—that is the key to physical and mental fitness.

As you consider your stuck situation, you can ask yourself the following questions to focus on the subjectivity of your thinking:

> What data have I noticed that led me to think as I do? What data have other people noticed, leading them to think as they do?

> How am I interpreting the data that I have? How might someone else interpret this data differently?

☛ What biases are coloring my thinking in this situation?

Remember that the Ladder of Inference is not for judging perspectives; it's for revealing them. We don't need to concede that we are wrong; rather, we need to always bear in mind that other people may be looking at things quite differently. Considering what data and interpretations led you to your conclusion, and doing likewise for the other side's conclusion, is a good habit to get into when you are facing a stuck dynamic. It is, in a sense, the antidote to perspective ignorance. And overcoming that will help you change your thinking and ultimately get you unstuck.

ACTIVE RESISTANCE

Resistance to seeing another perspective can be more aggressive than mere ignorance. Alex, who demanded a fourth new assistant from Holly in HR, flatly refused to consider that he was part of the problem and that he played a role in his stuck dynamic. Why?

Resistance is not simply a matter of "not getting it." That is, Alex can understand, in the abstract, a situation where a demanding and unreasonable manager keeps finding fault with his assistants, never recognizing that his standards are unrealistically high and that he might be expecting too much from his staff members before training them. Intellectually, that story makes sense. Alex just doesn't accept that that story has anything to do with him.

Well, why not? Isn't it obvious? I think it is obvious to any outsider. Someone who was truly neutral would of course recognize, upon getting feedback from an outsider (someone such as Holly) that he was contributing to this situation.

But Alex, like all of us, is not neutral in his story. He vigorously rejects the notion that he has any culpability here precisely because if he did, he'd have to recognize that *his* behavior was a problem. Embracing that other perspective would be uncomfortable, even painful.

The avoidance of this discomfort can be explained by a psychological phenomenon called *cognitive dissonance*.[3] It refers to the discomfort people feel when trying to hold conflicting or dissonant cognitions. Because of this discomfort, people strive to reduce the dissonance, frequently by rejecting the conflicting information. Alex believes many things about himself as a professional and as an individual: He is a fair person, he is a good communicator, he has reasonable expectations of people, he knows how to train people, and he is self-aware.

When confronted with his frustrating experience in which none of his assistants is able to continue working for him, Alex is put into a dilemma. On the one hand, he has a number of positive beliefs about himself. On the other hand, he knows that he is consistently having a hard time finding a good assistant. This poses an internal conflict creating cognitive dissonance. Alex wants to eliminate the dissonance, and so he decides that the feedback that he is a lousy manager or isn't taking time to train people is not true. Believing that the assistants being sent to him are of low quality avoids the dissonance, since Alex can maintain his highly positive self-image despite his recent frustrations. Problem solved. Or rather, the internal cognitive dissonance problem is now solved; the problem of finding an assistant remains and perhaps gets worse.

Moreover, this process happens subconsciously. It's not as if Alex says, "I'm going to consciously choose to disregard what Holly is telling me about myself because it's uncomfortable." He truly believes what he is saying. Of course, to an outsider, the reality is painfully obvious. But for the person inside the situation, his biased view feels completely accurate.

It would be wrong to think of Alex as exceptional in his reaction to Holly's feedback. We are all subject to biases in how we approach our stuck situations. These biases, which have been well documented by social psychologists, protect and enhance our self-image. For example, the well-known and aptly titled *self-serving bias* explains that people believe they deserve disproportionate personal credit for successes but allocate disproportionate blame to others for failures.[4] Doing so helps people maintain a positive self-image, which is a natural desire.

This natural desire, however, interferes with our ability to shift perspective. When something goes wrong at work, I will naturally assign blame to my colleague. My colleague, subject to the same bias in reverse, naturally assigns blame to me. As we try to discuss what happened, our conversation can easily deteriorate into a battle of recriminations and defenses, creating a stuck situation. For me to attempt to shift my thinking and see my colleague's perspective, I need to go against my natural ego-protecting, self-serving bias. Flexing my mind would require me to consider whether and how I did something to contribute to what went wrong at work. Doing so, while necessary for getting unstuck, is threatening and uncomfortable.

It is beyond the scope of this book to catalog all of the psychological defenses people use to avoid painful feelings and to preserve their self-image. But experience confirms that admitting one is wrong, acknowledging that one is at fault, or owning one's weaknesses are uncomfortable to do. Even considering these possibilities—which is what flexing your mind forces you to do—can be psychologically painful. This is why Alex, like most of us, does the opposite of flexing his mind. He tenses his mind, blocking out the other point of view and its uncomfortable implications.

Circumventing these psychological defenses is essential before a person can begin to flex his mind. But how? Consider the metaphor of a brick wall. If you were a military commander trying to get past an enemy's brick wall, the least effective way would be a frontal assault. Smashing into the wall won't work, because you will become exhausted or get shot down before you get through. In similar fashion, trying to smash through someone's psychological defenses usually doesn't work. Indeed, the harder you push, the more they push back. If Holly were to push harder and harder on Alex to admit that he is the problem, he will likely fight back harder and harder to prove that he is not. They would get even more stuck; Holly would feel that she tried everything and that Alex was impossible, and Alex would feel that Holly just blamed him because she didn't want to admit that her pool of assistants was subpar.

It would be far more effective to find a way to either get around the wall of the psychological barrier or else to chip away at it, one brick at a time. One way to circumvent the wall is not to fight against the defense mechanism. Consider the following dialogue:

Holly: Alex, let's assume that you are right that the quality of the assistants is indeed low, and that they are not able to learn as quickly as you have a right to expect. We are still stuck in this situation. What do you propose we do?

Alex: Attract higher-caliber candidates by paying them more money.

Holly: That is something to consider, although it would have to be approved by senior management. Approving and implementing that strategy could take quite a while.

Alex: Well, if we don't invest in attracting talented people we can't get better.

Holly: I know you would like to change the applicant pool. That's unlikely to happen in the short term. Another way of thinking is to consider what you can do to optimize things with the current applicant pool. Rightly or wrongly, if you can't change them, what can you do differently to make it better?

Alex: I don't know what you mean.

Holly: I know you are frustrated that people are not picking up on their own the way you like to have your calendar organized. What do you think of taking more time to train them?

Alex: I don't have the time.

Holly: We could arrange for the training to happen outside of normal business hours. Maybe you could spend a few hours with your assistant in the evening or on a weekend—that way it would not interfere with your regular work.

Alex: That's possible. But it's a shame we can't get better people in here who wouldn't need to be spoon-fed.

Holly: I know that is how you feel. But let's try this strategy and see how it goes.

In essence, Holly shouldn't fight against Alex's perspective; instead, she should embrace it. Reducing the emotional threat of seeing another perspective helps him relax and "unclench" his mind. When Alex does not feel threatened, he may be open to seeing other dimensions of the situation, or at least open to trying other strategies for solving it.

Depending on their relationship and on how successful Holly has been at reducing the emotional threat to Alex, she might try chipping away at the brick wall of his defenses. That would involve saying something such as, "Alex, let's assume that most of the problem is what you said. Let's assume that the quality of candidates is 90 percent of the issue. Are you open to considering that you might be contributing to 10 percent of the problem?" This remark leaves most of the defense intact, but is a bit more aggressive in that it openly invites Alex to begin considering another point of view.

We are all human, and we are all susceptible to biases and emotional defenses to shifting perspective. What can a person do, on her own, to fight against this strong tendency? Here are some practical suggestions for unclenching your mind:

> ➤ *Don't fight against your own defenses.* Allow yourself to assume you are 90 percent in the right in your situation; you can even assume you are 100 percent right. Ask yourself, nevertheless,

"What are some variables that I have control over—my own behavior, my own reactions, my own feelings—that I can modify in order to change this situation?" You may find that doing so helps you relax and, in turn, opens your mind to other perspectives.

▷ *Write down your perspective, and then write down the other side's perspective.* Putting things on paper helps create the detachment and distance that allows you to flex your mind.

▷ *List the benefits of seeing other perspectives.* This exercise can motivate you to try harder to flex your mind.

▷ *Describe your fears about seeing the other perspective.* Sometimes the best way to disarm a psychological defense is to get closer to it. Ask yourself, "What are my fears about seeing the other side's point of view?" Once you explicitly name the fear, it's easier to face it and to work on effectively navigating your stuck situation.

It is impossible to flex your mind while you clench it at the same time. Relaxing your mind, letting go of the desire to be right, and being willing to consider your own faults or mistakes, is the first step in shifting perspective.

An indispensable element of truly unclenching your mind is sincerity. George Burns once said that the "most important thing to succeed in show business is sincerity, and if you can fake that, you've got it made."[5] Faking sincerity is an oxymoron, of course; the essence of sincerity is that it is authentic. But this quote captures one of the challenges in striving for sincerity: How can I tell if I am authentically flexing my mind? How do I know if I am, in truth, open? Although shifting perspective doesn't mean you have to agree with the other point of view, you do have to flex your mind enough to embrace it, at least temporarily. You have to truly open yourself up to the other point of view and not just go through the motions. Pretending to be open without really being open won't help, and can actually make things worse.

I may think I have done the hard work of seeing the other person's perspective, but maybe I wasn't trying hard enough. Indeed, what is the difference between embracing another point of view and just going through the motions?

Here are three common pitfalls that can indicate that, perhaps, you have not gone all the way in flexing your mind.

Mean What You Say

Not long ago I was charged for something I did not purchase on my credit card bill, so I called the customer service number on the back of the card to get some help. As I began to explain my problem to the phone representative, I could sense how indifferent she was to my situation. If you were to read a transcript of the conversation, you would see that she said several times, "I'm sorry for the inconvenience." Yet notwithstanding the formulaic words (no doubt a scripted part of her training in customer service), her responses didn't make me feel understood. In fact, quite the opposite occurred. I got increasingly angry and felt completely disrespected. Why? Because although she used the word *sorry*, there was no real apology behind it. There was no real understanding or empathy for my situation, no real remorse, and no taking of responsibility. In fact, the phoniness of her words made them not only unhelpful, but outright harmful.

When you catch yourself saying things you don't really mean or expressing emotions you don't actually feel, you need to work harder at flexing your mind. We've all been on the receiving end of insincere apologies and expressions of remorse. Even the right words, such as "I'm sorry," won't work when delivered without conviction. The only way for the right words to work is to mean them. And the only way to really mean them is to change your thinking—hence the importance of shifting perspective in changing your stuck situations.

As listeners, we can tell when someone is being insincere with us. But can the person who is speaking insincerely tell as well? I think so. I'm willing to bet that if you got that customer service representative to speak openly, she would admit that in her heart she wasn't truly sorry. In the example in Chapter Two, Kent, the attorney, was able to acknowledge he did not feel empathy for his clients, and he could even explain why—until his eye-opening experience with his doctor, of course.

To be fair to the customer service representative and everyone else who sometimes says things and doesn't mean it, there is a reason that this happens. Nodding one's head in a show of attentiveness is much easier than *actually* being attentive. Saying "sorry" is a lot easier than actually being sorry. Saying "I empathize" is a lot easier than actually empathizing. Sure, these shortcuts don't in fact work, but they are so tempting.

If you want a great example of people who no longer have the energy to be sincere, go to the airport and observe the airline staff. The gate attendants and flight attendants work in an industry that has been through tremendous challenges; they have seen their salaries and benefits cut, they work long hours on erratic schedules, and they have to handle more passengers with fewer staff members. They are worn out. And so while they may know the acceptable language to use with customers, there isn't a lot of sincerity behind their words. To me, they are like soldiers who have been left on the front lines for too long. Research done during World War II indicated that even experienced, effective infantry units can only remain on the front lines facing the enemy for so long. Performance peaks in the first ninety days of combat. After that effectiveness begins to deteriorate, and after between 140 and 180 days of continuous combat a soldier was basically useless in combat.[6] Past that point, they are no longer actually soldiers, but individuals who are just trying to get through the day and survive. That's why the military must rotate these units off the front lines to the rear, allow them some time to recuperate, and then bring them back to the front, refreshed and ready again to meet the enemy.

Although airports are not quite as stressful as wartime terrain, airline staff members spend far more than ninety days on the front line. Over time the stresses wear them out, and they become fatigued and incapable of doing their jobs properly. Retreating to buzzwords and superficial apologies is a natural survival strategy, albeit one that every passenger detests.

An unfortunate consequence of all of the scripting that happens with customer service representatives is that the currency of words has become devalued. When there are so many insincere "sorrys" being thrown around, the word becomes worthless. Then, when representatives are truly sorry, they need to find other ways to communicate that to their customers because the words have been overused and abused.

If you suspect you are just saying words without sincerity in your own stuck situations, that's a good sign that you need to work harder on flexing your mind. It's not difficult to tell when someone else is being insincere and just saying words without meaning them. To check your own behavior, simply flip it around by asking yourself, "If I were the other person and someone said this to me, would I believe it?" When reflecting on the possible gap between what you are saying and what is in your head, you can ask yourself, "What do I really think? What do I really feel? Do I mean the words I am saying?" Meaning what you say is an important part of changing your stuck dynamic. In the words of Johann Wolfgang von Goethe, the famous German writer of the late eighteenth and early nineteenth century, "What is uttered from the heart alone, will win the hearts of others to your own."[7]

Change Behavior in Macro, Not Just Micro, Ways

Sometimes you receive feedback that asks you to make a behavior change. You may find it's crucial and difficult to change your behavior, and not only in the specific "micro" context—you must also address the underlying "macro" problem.

Sacha was a marketing manager for a consumer products company. Although Sacha had many strengths, one problem area was her participation in group meetings—or rather, her lack of participation. She would often give only partial attention to the group, checking her e-mail while other people spoke. She was communicating to the people around her that she was not interested in what they were saying, so her manager asked her to stop checking e-mails and to engage more fully in the meetings. Sacha responded by saying that she understood and promised to change her behavior.

Sacha did indeed stop checking her e-mail in group meetings. However, this change did not make Sacha's colleagues feel much better toward her. Although she had stopped the specific behavior, Sacha hadn't taken in the underlying feedback—she was still not tuned in to meetings. Her mind would wander, and when people would ask for her input she would reply with comments such as, "I'm sorry, I wasn't paying attention. What was the question?"

Clearly, Sacha was still not engaging in meetings with her coworkers. The micro feedback she heard—"don't check e-mail"—was only one manifestation of the macro feedback—"participate in the meetings." Sacha had ceased checking e-mail, but she did not actually take on the request more generally to pay attention and participate in meetings. Why not? Clearly Sacha's perspective had not shifted, and she remained uninterested in what the group was discussing. Perhaps she felt that these meetings only deserved her partial attention, since they took too long. Maybe she felt she did not belong at these meetings since they were not relevant to her work. Regardless, what's clear is that Sacha's mindset remained unchanged, and so her dynamic with her coworkers also remained unchanged. Notwithstanding this one behavioral adjustment, things did not get better.

When you find yourself in a stuck situation and your counterpart is asking you to change what you do, don't be content with just changing your behavior. Consider the perspective of your counterpart and why the other person is asking for this behavioral change. If you understand the "why" behind the request, and you feel comfortable doing it (even if you disagree and/or consider the change a compromise), then that is a sign that you've at least seen the other person's perspective. Ask yourself, "Do I understand and accept the reason behind this request?" If you don't, you may find that your changed behavior is not changing the dynamic, and you need to reexamine your thinking.

Don't Avoid a Discussion of Gaps in Perspective

Shifting perspective doesn't mean you necessarily agree with the other side's point of view. But it does require that you try to see the other perspective, and if you profoundly disagree with it and cannot bridge the disagreement, saying so. Pretending to accept the other perspective is unlikely to make things better.

James and Dina were partners, cofounders of a ten-person design firm. As the economy worsened, James and Dina realized that they needed to cut costs to remain solvent. They agreed to eliminate two staff members, but had been battling over which workers to let go. James had suggested a number of individuals to lay off, but Dina rejected each one for various reasons. Their disagreement had caused paralysis, and no decisions about cost-cutting had been made at all. James, who was becoming worried that their inactivity might lead to the firm's demise, asked me to speak with Dina to see if I could help. We had the following conversation:

Me: How would you describe the issue between you and James?

Dina: It's pretty simple. We both recognize that we need to cut costs, and James explained that the biggest cost in our budget is staff salaries and benefits. I completely understand that we need to cut, but I am just having a hard time deciding who to let go.

Me: Why?

Dina: Well, I've been thinking about it a lot. And each person we've considered laying off is important to the firm. I keep thinking about how the firm will suffer without that person's contribution.

Me: It sounds like a tough choice. But won't the firm suffer more if you don't lay off some people?

Dina: That's what James keeps saying. I don't know if that's true, although James is convinced.

Me: Well, let's put James's view aside for a moment. What do you think?

Dina: I don't know. I guess I have my doubts.

Me: What are your doubts?

Dina: I was thinking that maybe we shouldn't lay off anyone at all, but instead should cut everyone's salaries by 10 percent. That would reduce our expenses but not harm the quality of our product.

Me: That might work.

Dina: That's what I think. But I made the suggestion to James, and he would not even discuss it.

Me: Why not?

Dina: He said, "Cutting salaries jeopardizes the firm even more. It will set the stage for people to leave quickly when they are offered more pay somewhere else. Everyone knows that you don't cut people's salaries." He was adamant that we need to lay people off and not burden the entire staff with the budget issues.

Me: And what do you think of that?

Dina: I've tried to defer to him on these matters, since he has more business experience than I do. But I'm struggling to make the right choice on who to fire.

Me: It sounds to me as if you are not convinced about the merits of firing people. Maybe that is why you are dragging your feet on making this tough choice.

Dina: Well, I know we need to cut costs. There's no question about that.

Me: True. But there are different ways of doing it. And my suspicion is that, because you have such deep doubts about the strategy, you are having a hard time putting it into effect.

Dina: You might be right.

Dina was able to describe what James wanted her to do, and she was able to do a decent job of explaining his rationale. She was also trying hard to make the tough choice, despite her ambivalence. So what was missing?

What was missing was a robust discussion between James and Dina about their differing perspectives. Dina had agreed to a course of action and was trying to follow through on it. But without hashing it out with James, she was not truly committed to it. Put simply, her heart was not in it. And pushing her harder to make the choice was not where the focus should be.

Dina and James needed to discuss their views more fully. Perhaps a compromise that everyone could live with could be found. Perhaps, after robust discussion, one of them would change his or her mind. But at this point, they needed to have a greater flexing of minds in order to reach a true meeting of the minds, after which they could jointly decide on a course of action.

In your own stuck situation, here are some questions to ask yourself:

> ➢ Have I had a chance to seriously discuss the differences in how my counterpart and I see things?

> Have I been able to bridge the gaps in perspective between me and my counterpart enough to really invest in this outcome?

> Am I committed to what I/we are doing?

If the answer is no, then you need to go back and discuss your perspectives some more. More exploration of the other side's point of view might lead to a better outcome, or at least a realization that your goals may be incompatible.

SUMMARY

Seeing another perspective is deeply challenging; it takes effort. When left to our own devices, we either "don't know" or "don't care" about other perspectives. We all need to work hard to flex our minds, because seeing another perspective can be psychological painful and, as such, it is something we tend to avoid. But if you are reading this book, it's because you want to shift your stuck situation. In the words of Albert Einstein, "We cannot solve our problems with the same thinking we used when we created them."[8] Although thinking differently takes work, it's the only way. And doing that with sincerity requires moving toward the challenge of seeing other points of view, not away from it. The next three chapters are going to show you how.

CHAPTER 4

Tell Their Story

LOOKING THROUGH THEIR EYES

I once managed a talented employee named Evan. Evan was good at his job, and in general, I enjoyed working with him. But whenever a problem or difficult topic would come up between us, Evan simply shut down. I would share my thoughts, and he would listen politely. When I asked for his input, he responded with bland answers such as, "I think you made good points," or "That makes sense," or "I'll think about what you said." The more I tried to talk to him, the more Evan retreated and avoided me.

In my mind, Evan was the problem. After all, I consistently tried to engage him, as any responsible colleague would; he was the one preventing us from talking. Although thinking this way did not help me solve my problem communicating with Evan, at least it made me feel better. Evan had issues; the situation was not my fault.

After this dynamic persisted for a while, I reached out to a colleague for advice. When I described my frustration to her, she said, "Maybe Evan is uncomfortable. You put him on the spot, and it may be that he is just a gentler and more polite person than you. Plus, as his manager, you may be intimidating to him. Try taking a different approach."

Her comment forced me, for the first time, to pause and consider the situation from Evan's point of view. When I did that, it was as if a veil had been lifted. Of course Evan shut down; that's because his style was so radically different from mine. Part of Evan's charm, and the reason he was beloved by all, was his agreeable nature. His natural tendency in the face of disagreement was to try to smooth things over. I, on the other hand, reacted to disagreement by "digging in" and trying to get to the core of the issue. It was a toxic combination. My aggressive engagement inevitably pushed him farther away. I reacted, predictably, with even more tenacious attempts to engage, fostering more evasion on his part, and this vicious cycle had created my frustrating situation. As I continued to try to tell Evan's story—that is, describe the situation as he would—I could see the importance of hierarchy as well. For Evan, I was not just someone he worked with; I was his boss. Of course, the power imbalance between manager and subordinate greatly magnified Evan's reluctance to engage in a confrontation.

Once I saw the situation through Evan's eyes, and how upsetting it was for Evan to be repeatedly confronted by an aggressive boss intent on pushing him into a difficult conversation before he was ready, I said to myself, *Now I get it.*

This skill—the skill of telling the other person's story as the individual would himself—is the topic of this chapter.

DIFFERENCE OF OPINION

Consider the following statement: People are different from me, and their point of view is as legitimate as mine. There are two parts to this sentence, each of which will be addressed.

People are different. "So what?" you say. That's obvious. In fact, it is beyond obvious. Diversity is a cherished value in most

Western democratic societies. Differences in taste, opinion, belief, thinking, faith, and values are embraced. Society conditions us not only to acknowledge people's differences, but to celebrate them.

Now consider the following story: You meet a new friend named Tom and invite him over for a small dinner party together with some other guests. At the party, the guests are all mingling and chatting and having a nice time. The party is going quite well.

The conversation turns to politics. Among your group of friends, many different political leanings are represented. Because of the sensitivity of the topic, everyone tries to be respectful. Everyone except Tom, that is. He dominates the conversation, talking for long stretches without pausing. While someone else is talking, Tom rudely interrupts with a comment to rebut the speaker. He is dismissive of others' viewpoints. He raises his voice at times. Several guests seem visibly uncomfortable with Tom's aggressive tone, and even you are becoming embarrassed. You try a few times to subtly steer the discussion to other subjects, hoping to defuse the situation, but Tom seems not to notice. The conversation does not shift until you bring out dessert, at which point everyone seems tired of arguing and your strawberry shortcake becomes the primary topic of conversation.

After the party, you are upset and angry. You feel betrayed by Tom. You don't know him that well, yet you invited him into your home and your circle of friends. He repays your hospitality with rudeness and embarrassment. You resolve never to invite him to your house again.

The story could end here. What happened is clear—your guest was rude and inappropriate. Your anger is justified, given your understanding of what happened.

But wait! What happened to remembering that people are different? Isn't it possible that Tom simply has a different style than you do? Isn't it possible that his behavior wasn't rude at all, but that you misunderstood him?

No, you reply. This is an extreme and clear-cut case. There is simply no excuse for that kind of rudeness. While it's important to recognize that people are different, that doesn't excuse Tom's aggressive behavior while a guest in someone's home.

Before continuing the story of Tom, let's pause and reflect. In this moment you are stuck because you are forgetting that people are different. People behave as they do for many different reasons, and there are many ways to interpret people's actions. It's unlikely that Tom simply considers himself a rude person who enjoys antagonizing acquaintances and new friends. Yet even the most well-intentioned people—such as people who are committed to diversity—tend to forget that people truly are different, and thus they don't even begin the search for alternative explanations for the behavior of someone such as Tom. And this matters, because it is at these moments that people get stuck, and it is precisely in moments like these that people need to flex their minds and strive to look at the situation through the other person's eyes.

Now, to get back to the story. . . .

Assuming you are willing to reconsider your initial reaction, you can start to explore other possibilities. Why would Tom, who seemed like such a good guy and who was happy to have been invited to your home, act the way he did? Is there some other explanation for what happened?

In your process of reflection on the party and Tom's participation, you might recall that Tom is from Israel. And you may further note that Israeli culture differs dramatically from American culture in that it is far more confrontational. Conversations have a different rhythm; interrupting another person, for example, is commonplace, even expected, and typically does not give offense (although some speakers may not consent to the interruption and simply keep talking over an interrupter until they have finished what they wanted to say). When the topic is politics, these traits are magnified. In Israel, discussing politics is not taboo; rather, it is practically a national sport. When talking or arguing about politics, Israelis are comfortable adopting an aggressive stance, using what non-Israelis might consider a rude tone in their speech and even raising their voices.

Given all of these factors, you may reconsider whether Tom is rude, or whether he simply behaved using a different set of cultural norms. Indeed, within his culture, his behavior was entirely appropriate. Taking this line of thinking even further, Tom may have felt that the *other* guests were rude for not engaging authentically, and he may have been offended that they did not consider him a worthy interlocutor and share their true, unbridled sentiments when discussing politics.

Having explored these possibilities, you can now choose to have a conversation with Tom about what happened at the party, a conversation that both respects and explores Tom's perspective, which may be different from yours, while also sharing your own.

This story illustrates two important points. First, while it may be obvious that people are different, it's hard to remember that when you're in the middle of a stuck situation. The recognition that people are different, and the effort to understand the other person's story, are pushed aside. Instead, we treat our own story as "what really happened" and our reaction as based on "reality."[1] We then judge the other person according to our own framework. This is what happened with Tom. Indeed, people resist exploring differences when faced with conflict. The instinctual response to the suggestion that Tom may have behaved the way he did because he is different is "That's no excuse for his behavior."

Thus, we need to make a habit of pausing and actively flexing our mind, reflecting on how the other person may have viewed the situation. That is, when confronted with a challenging situation, we must consciously look for ways the other person may be different from us and then view the situation through the other person's eyes. Practice is essential for building the flexibility of mind needed to overcome the instinctual response of justifying our own narrative.

Second, the story reinforces an important point mentioned in Chapter Two: Flexing one's mind and exploring differences can, in a moment of conflict, help people handle a situation more constructively. Consider the following: Do you feel differently about Tom and his behavior at the party after reading the paragraph about Israeli culture? Does thinking about your and Tom's different styles and expectations of appropriate behavior change how you would discuss the party with him? I believe the answer to both questions is yes. The angry host who does not consider Tom's perspective will either avoid Tom or self-righteously accuse him of ruining the dinner party. However, someone who actively considers Tom's perspective and tries to tell his story can discuss the party calmly, with much greater openness to learning and problem solving than would otherwise be possible.

THE ROLE OF CULTURE

The story of Tom is one of culture as a source of differences between people. Culture, which we can define as learned human behavior patterns acquired by individuals as members of society, is indeed a powerful force that governs how people interact. It is a significant part of the subjective lens through which we look at the world. It shapes both Tom's expectations and definition of proper behavior, and our own interpretation of what Tom says and does.

Culture is far from the only source of diversity. Style, personality, age, gender, and organizational role are among the many other factors that matter as well. Nevertheless, looking for cultural differences is a good place to start. Why? Because culture is something we can easily point to and discuss. Understanding someone else's culture can be difficult; but understanding that someone *has* a culture that may differ from ours is easy. Even if you don't know a thing about Israeli culture, it is not hard to imagine how that could have shaped everything Tom did at the party that upset you. Moreover, once culture is on the table, you can talk about it explicitly. You can discuss with Tom, in a depersonalized and nonjudgmental manner, how people talk about politics in the United States and how it differs from the custom in Israel. (As we will see later, talking about someone's personality in this way can be a bit harder.)

In a global economy, where people regularly interact with colleagues and customers from around the world, sensitivity to cultural differences is essential. Let's consider an example: You are a member of an internal audit group for a large American corporation and you're based in headquarters. Monitoring the compliance procedures of different departments around the company is one of your primary responsibilities. In the course of performing your job, you write an e-mail to Mina, a colleague in the IT department, based in India, asking her to provide some documentation on various projects that were completed this year. Mina e-mails back that she will send you the documentation as soon as possible.

Several days go by and nothing happens. You send Mina another e-mail, asking for an update on her progress, but get no response. You then call Mina, asking for a status report. She replies that she is working on getting the documentation, but that it's taking a little longer than she expected. She promises to get you the information soon. A few more days go by and you still get no response. Exasperated, you write another e-mail, this time copying your and Mina's respective managers, reiterating that you are still waiting for the requested report. The next day Mina e-mails you back, saying she has arranged a conference call between you and her manager to discuss the requested documentation.

How do you understand this story? If you are an American accustomed to working in the American corporate context, it's a clear case of a colleague not doing her job. A legitimate request for documentation was sent, and Mina said she would take care of it. She consistently delayed, and avoided sending the information requested. If there were problems in procuring the material that required her manager's involvement, Mina should have stated that up front, which would have saved time and hassle. The story seems quite straightforward.

Let's consider the story from Mina's vantage point.

First of all, Mina is located in the company's Bangalore office in India, and she is operating within their local culture. This is an important consideration, because cultural norms matter and affect communication patterns.

Second, the requested documentation is, in fact, not available. Mina investigated the matter, and it turns out that various senior staff members have been lax in documenting their procedures. While this lack of documentation is not Mina's fault, it does put her in a difficult position. What is the appropriate way for her to handle this difficulty?

It would not be appropriate for Mina to simply say to her American colleague, "Senior staff members here have not done their jobs properly." While in the States, this response might be considered laudable honesty, in India it would embarrass her superiors and is unacceptable. At the same time, Mina does not want to be dishonest and tell a colleague the information is available when it's not. That is also not appropriate. Thus, she is in a bind.

A difficult conversation between someone in the Bangalore IT office and someone from your audit department needs to happen, but at a more senior level. In the meantime, while you wait for a response from IT, Mina can probably do no more than suggest or request that someone help her respond to you. She cannot demand that someone senior in her group respond to your e-mails. So, what can Mina do? She must delay in order not to upset or offend anyone, until the right response can be delivered. Her evasive replies, while potentially frustrating, are actually designed to send a subtle message to you that something is going on, without giving offense or causing embarrassment to her senior colleagues. Indeed, if a fellow worker in India were to receive similar responses, he would likely read between the lines and perceive that there is some difficulty that is not being addressed head-on. An Indian colleague might then try to engage in a phone conversation and gently probe Mina for more information, or she might simply try to solve the problem through other means (e.g., speak with other people in the department). What is clear is that someone who understood the cultural context would experience less frustration and probably would react less aggressively.

Told from the Mina's point of view, the story now reads quite differently. Identifying the cultural norms that created misunderstanding allows for the possibility of more constructive communication.

Getting everyone on the same page, particularly in a global economy, often requires deep sensitivity to cultural norms and differences. When someone's behavior or reaction to a situation doesn't make sense, make it a habit to flex your mind by asking yourself, "Is there a culture gap here?" As the examples of both Tom and Mina show, paying attention to diversity can save you much aggravation and misunderstanding. And once you have identified a culture gap, you can raise the topic in a neutral and nonjudgmental way.

IDENTIFYING NONCULTURAL DIFFERENCES

Culture, while important, isn't everything. People's personalities, experiences, training, and education are all sources of diversity. These types of differences are often more subtle, and spotting them in action can be quite difficult. In addition, the resistance to seeing the other side's point of view is often much greater.

Penelope and Mary work together in a small office. They spend significant time interacting with each other every day and are usually quite friendly. While Penelope respects Mary as a professional and a colleague, she finds it awkward to be around her. The issue is that Mary consistently asks Penelope all sorts of personal questions, such as, "How are things with your significant other?" or "Are you close with your family?" or "Was your pregnancy planned?" Penelope feels these questions are inappropriate, and that they do not respect her privacy. She experiences Mary as violating the boundaries between co-workers.

When asked why Mary behaves this way, Penelope says, "I think she is trying to pry into my private life. She is a nosy individual who wants to have the latest gossip."

But Mary has a story of her own. Mary is a warm and open person. She loves to connect with people—family and friends alike—and her way of drawing close is to have intimate conversations about whatever is going on in her life. Mary is quite fond of Penelope and would like to be closer to her. Thus, Mary both asks Penelope about her life and shares details of her own life with Penelope. She often tells Penelope about her weekend plans, her love interests, and her family history. Mary is frustrated, because she feels that despite her best efforts, Penelope has been strangely resistant to building a personal relationship with her, even though they work together very well. In response, Mary has been trying even harder to get close to Penelope, as a way of strengthening their relationship.

So who is right? The point here, of course, is that neither woman is right or wrong; these women are simply different, although you probably identify more with one character than the other. In this case, it's a difference not of culture, but of personality. Moreover, Penelope does not frame her discomfort with Mary in terms of how different Mary is, and so she interprets Mary's behavior using her own frame of reference. Penelope might feel differently about Mary's behavior if she were able to understand that the behavior is Mary's way of drawing close.

In my experience with Evan (as described at the beginning of this chapter), I felt differently about our conversations after I reflected on how he would describe the situation. I became less judgmental, less angry, and in general more open-minded. But that was only the first step. My newfound awareness made it clear to me that I needed to discuss things with Evan so that we could try to find a dynamic that would work better.

I sat down for a conversation with Evan and broached the subject of discussing our different styles of communication. I explained that I tended to be quite direct, even aggressive, when raising difficult issues, and I suggested that maybe this approach was uncomfortable for him. I asked Evan to give me some advice and guidance on how to adapt my style to make him more comfortable having these kinds of conversations.

Much to my surprise, Evan opened up. He said that he, too, found our conversations challenging. He often felt pressured into talking to me. In particular, he said, when there were delicate topics to discuss, such as constructive criticism, he felt that I demanded that he engage immediately, instead of giving him time to reflect and process his own thoughts and feelings. And so, when forced into having a conversation he did not want to have, he would usually listen and not respond, since he did not yet know what he wanted to say. Evan suggested that our conversations would be much more productive if I would allow him to consider my comments and then further discuss them with me at a later time. We had a productive discussion of our different styles, and I offered to try adapting my approach to make it easier for him to engage.

Afterward, when I reflected on our exchange, I was surprised by how differently Evan had been experiencing our conversations. For me, the most natural and productive means of getting through a tough topic is to press for immediate discussion, which is what I did. Thus, I experienced Evan as avoiding discussion. In contrast, for Evan, the most natural and productive means of dealing with a tough topic was also through conversation, but at a slower and more measured pace that left him time to think and process his feelings. It had never occurred to me just how different Evan's style was from mine. And had our differences not come to light, our relationship would have continued to deteriorate. Once I considered Evan's perspective, I realized that I could and should adapt my approach so that he would be able to engage with me. The crucial first step in the process was recognizing that Evan and I were different, and his experience of our conversations was vastly different from mine.

DIFFERENT AND LEGITIMATE

When dealing with difference, people face an additional challenge. Recognizing that the other person is different is not enough. To truly make situations go better, one needs to see that another person's perspective is not only different, but also *legitimate*.

There's even a joke that makes this point: Two clergymen are arguing about theology and how to worship God, with neither able to convince the other that his position is the right one. Finally, one man turns to his colleague and says, "Look, we don't have to agree on everything. You can go worship God your way, and I will worship him His way."

The joke, of course, is that under the guise of open-mindedness, the clergyman who made the comment is actually asserting hierarchy and manifesting a patronizing attitude to his colleague. Implied in his statement is, "My way is the right way; however, I will indulge your wrong way because I am tolerant."

Why is it so important to accord legitimacy to the other person's point of view? For three reasons: 1) to bridge the gap, 2) to truly understand the other person's perspective, and 3) to avoid appearing condescending.

First, without giving the other viewpoint at least a bit of legitimacy, there is no motivation to bridge the gap. Let's say, for example, that I get as far as recognizing that Evan's style and his experience of our conversations are different from mine. But once I see the difference, I could simply say, "Well, the fact that Evan can't handle direct conversations is his problem. If he wants to work with me, he'll have to adapt." At that point, I have exempted myself from any effort to improve the situation. It's Evan's problem, and, by extension, it's something that only Evan can solve. This way of thinking is seductive for precisely that reason—it lets me off the hook. I don't need to feel bad about my deteriorating relationship with my colleague because it's *his* problem. He's the one with the weird communication hang-up who can't tolerate conflict; I'm just a normal guy who likes to have honest conversations. While this may feel good to you, it is a sure recipe to stay locked in your stuck situation.

Keep in mind the point that was made in Chapter Two: There can be more than one legitimate point of view. It's not a matter of either Evan's style *or* my style being legitimate. Rather, both Evan's style *and* my style can be legitimate, and our shared goal is to bridge the gap between us.

Second, in order to truly understand another person's perspective, one has to start by suspending judgment and giving it legitimacy. Why? Because until we do, we cannot truly understand the other side. The ultimate goal is to understand the other person's story from the inside—that is, from inside how that person sees it. But on the inside, an individual's story *is* legitimate. Evan doesn't believe that slowing down the conversation is a bad way to communicate; on the contrary, to him, it is the most natural and respectful thing to do. Tom, the Israeli guest, doesn't think that aggressively talking politics is rude and inappropriate at an American dinner party; on the contrary, he feels it is rude not to be totally honest in what one is thinking. For Mary, sharing and asking about intimate details of one's life with a coworker isn't nosy; it's how people show they care. We have to let go of our desire for our way to be the "right" way and explore someone else's "right way." We need to set aside judgment, if only temporarily, to understand the other side's perspective.

That doesn't mean that I have to ultimately think the other person's way is better than mine, or even as good. But to get into someone else's head, I need to explore that person's view with an open attitude that asks, "How can this perspective make the most sense to the person who believes it?" It's hard to do, but not impossible.

The final reason for giving another person's view legitimacy is quite practical—if I don't, I am likely to appear condescending and patronizing. If, when talking to Evan, I had not set aside the feeling of being right, I might have begun our conversation by saying, "Look, I know you are uncomfortable with conflict and with difficult topics, so I will try to accommodate that." While the words seem conciliatory, the underlying message is, "Your way is wrong; I will try to indulge you." This type of patronizing attitude is actually a barrier to understanding the perspective. It does not facilitate constructive dialogue, and Evan is not likely to open up to me as a result. Instead, I said, "I think we have really different styles, and I'd like to find a way to bridge the gap so that we are both comfortable having tough conversations." The message here is, "Your way is as right to you as mine is to me." *That* is acknowledging that Evan's perspective is both different and legitimate, and it facilitates getting unstuck.

MIND THE GAP

Suspending judgment is essential for bridging the gap between how we see the world and how our counterpart sees it. But it is by no means easy. As mentioned in Chapter Three, shifting perspective is something people tend to resist. And the greater the gap in perspectives, the greater the resistance. That is, when it comes to looking at the situation from the other side's point of view, the difficulty in shifting perspective is proportional to the gap between the parties.

The challenge is greater on two levels. First, the sheer size of the gap makes bridging it harder. The more direct I am in my style, the harder it is for me to relate to Evan's indirect style. The more private Penelope is in her work relationships, the more difficult it is for her to see good intentions in Mary's invasive questions. The more individualistic and outspoken I am as an American corporate citizen, the harder it is for me to imagine how things look to someone from India with vastly different corporate norms.

In addition, the more different the other perspective is, the more *threatening* it is to accord it legitimacy. For me to see Evan's perspective, I also need to see myself through his eyes. And what emerges is a less-than-flattering portrait of a pushy, overbearing, and even controlling boss. I'd rather not see that view when it's much more comfortable for me to simply declare Evan the problem. For Penelope to see Mary's questions as warm and inviting, rather than intrusive, she might have to see herself as uptight and closed. It's much more comfortable for her is to simply see Mary as nosy. But doing that won't get me or Penelope unstuck.

PRACTICE TELLING THEIR STORY

So far we've learned that it is difficult to see the other person's point of view, particularly in cases where the two parties have different cultural paradigms, personalities, or expectations. The difficulty of remembering that people are different is, moreover, exacerbated in moments of conflict. In such cases, people tend not to see the other side's perspective. Furthermore, when they do, it's often with a patronizing attitude: "I understand their perspective—it's just wrong." All of this makes having constructive conversations difficult.

There is, however, a way to improve at seeing the other person's point of view, even when in conflict. I call this method "Telling Their Story."

Telling their story sounds easy—it simply means narrating the situation or conflict from the point of view of the other side. Yet, even when people try it, their own point of view constantly seeps in, making it challenging. Thus, we need to practice telling their story, not in a neutral way, but in a "reverse-biased" way that *favors the other side*. We need to tell their story as they would tell it themselves. Practicing this method cultivates a flexible mind and is extremely helpful in shifting perspective and facilitating constructive conversations.

For example, Sam, a coaching client, asked me for help in dealing with his colleague Chris.[2] He and Chris frequently collaborated on various projects, but Chris always waited until the last minute before finishing anything, not realizing or caring that his delays created stress for other people, particularly for Sam. He had tried to discuss the situation with Chris, Sam told me, but it went poorly. We chatted about his interactions with his colleague until I felt I had a reasonable understanding of Chris's point of view. I then suggested that we role-play his conversation with Chris, with me playing Chris and Sam playing himself. The role-played conversation went as follows:

Sam: Chris, I need to talk to you about how we work together. You always wait until the last minute to get things done, and that's not acceptable.

Me (as Chris): I always get things done on time. I prefer to wait until I know exactly what the client wants before I invest too much effort. Overplanning is a waste of time. Besides, I have other things that I could be doing instead.

Sam: But it's inefficient, and it's not fair to everyone else.

Me (as Chris): I find it to be extremely efficient. I don't like working so far in advance of a deadline; I don't focus as well. It's not fair to ask me to work on your schedule.

Sam: It's not my schedule, it's just acting professionally. You're being completely self-centered.

At this point I stopped the conversation and asked Sam if I was saying the kinds of things that Chris tended to say, and he replied, "Yes, he says almost exactly those words." I asked Sam if he understood Chris's point of view, and he said, "Of course I do; I hear it over and over. For six months, I have been listening to nothing else." I asked Sam to summarize Chris's point of view, and he said, "Chris doesn't like to plan things, and he refuses to. And that is insensitive and self-centered." I asked him if he thought it was that simple, and Sam said, "Look, this isn't a complex issue. He needs to be a team player and work on a schedule that works for everyone, not just for him. It really is that simple."

Let's pause this story and analyze. Clearly, Sam is failing miserably at understanding Chris's perspective. He oversimplifies Chris's story and strips away almost all the nuances of what Chris actually said. In Chris's own story, he articulates several reasons for not wanting to plan: He feels that planning too far in advance is inefficient, making it harder for him to focus. He enjoys the flexibility of not "overplanning" and feels his time can be more efficiently used on other things. And, Chris explains, he feels Sam is trying to force him to work on Sam's schedule.

Yet in Sam's *description* of Chris, there is no acknowledgment of any of these points. For Sam, it's simple: "Chris is insensitive and self-centered."

Furthermore, to the extent Sam understands Chris at all, he certainly doesn't see Chris's view as legitimate. The negative terms he uses to describe Chris—*insensitive* and *self-centered*—make that clear as well.

Biased, erroneous, and oversimplified descriptions of the other side's narrative are common. Children can be wonderfully blunt in how they describe the other side. When asked why a strict teacher assigns so much homework, children commonly say, "Because he is mean," or "Because she hates the students." This kind of response is to be expected from a child, but the dynamic occurs with adults as well, especially when adults are regressing into childlike behavior, as they may do in stuck situations. When we don't like what someone is doing, we assign that individual a simplistic role in an oversimplified narrative: "He simply doesn't like to plan." "She is insensitive." "He is controlling." "She is selfish."

Sam's description of his interaction with Chris is striking in yet another way. When asked, Sam asserts that he understands Chris's story very well. He insists that his (oversimplified and critical) description of Chris's perspective accurately captures what Chris thinks. To the outside observer, someone who is not directly affected by the situation and not threatened by what Chris is saying, this description of Chris's point of view is obviously inaccurate. But it's not only that Sam misses the nuances in Chris's story; he is also *unaware* that he missed these nuances. Quite the contrary: When probed, Sam declares his certainty that he has fully understood Chris. He is totally oblivious to how much he has failed to understand.

I refer to this phenomenon as *nested unawareness,* which is being unaware of the other person's point of view and, additionally, being unaware of being unaware. Nested unawareness presents a formidable barrier to getting unstuck, because it closes one's mind to even considering a different understanding of the other side's point of view. Why should Sam push himself to explore Chris's perspective when he already gets it?

Thus, the first step toward getting unstuck is uncertainty. It is essential to cultivate a stance of uncertainty and to maintain constant openness to the possibility that we have misunderstood or mischaracterized our counterpart's perspective. Before any progress can be made with Sam, he needs to open his mind to alternative narratives for Chris, beyond declaring that "Chris is insensitive and self-centered."

But it's far from easy. A stance of uncertainty requires giving up the comfort of being right. And, as we have seen, the more different the other side's perspective, the more uncomfortable it is to be open to that perspective.

I confronted Sam about his oversimplification of Chris's narrative and invited him to see things as Chris might, explaining that while Sam believes his method of scheduling work is objectively professional, Chris sees it as Sam trying to impose his work style on Chris. And for Chris, Sam's planning is just as frustrating as Chris's laid-back attitude is to Sam. For Chris, Sam seems like a rigid, inflexible overplanner. I pushed Sam to see Chris's view as different and legitimate, at least in Chris's eyes.

Sam begrudgingly listened and then protested, "But Chris is wrong! Why should I legitimize a view I think is completely unreasonable?"

My response to Sam, to recap what was described earlier in this chapter, was simply that understanding the other point of view will help Sam improve the situation. It will allow Sam to have a more constructive conversation. I also emphasized that Sam does not need to adopt Chris's view, merely to understand it. Sam doesn't need to become like Chris in order to work more effectively with Chris. What he needs to do is to learn to communicate with Chris more effectively about their different styles and needs.

Following this discussion of the importance of understanding where Chris was coming from, I asked Sam to try to summarize his colleague's point of view. He said, "I guess Chris feels that I am trying to force him to do things my way, which means planning. And he doesn't like to plan. So he probably feels that not only am I asking him to do something he doesn't like to do, but I am forcing it on him by saying, 'It's the only legitimate way to do things,' rather than asking him to do it for the benefit of the company."

At this point I knew we were making progress. Sam was beginning to set aside his own viewpoint; he was willing to see Chris's point of view as different *and* legitimate. I then said to Sam, "So if you were a reasonable person with Chris's viewpoint, what would you want?" And Sam, after thinking for a minute, said, "I guess I would want the other person to listen to me and respect my point of view. And I would want to feel that I'm choosing to compromise by doing more planning than I'd like, as opposed to being forced into changing my natural work style."

Sam was now starting to see Chris's story from the inside, describing his colleague's perspective in a much more robust and nuanced way. The contrast with Sam's original description of Chris's story was striking. This shift in his thinking became possible when Sam put himself in Chris's shoes and deliberately tried to tell his story as Chris would himself.

The change in Sam's attitude toward Chris and their differences set the stage for a different, more constructive conversation. I invited Sam to try role-playing a new conversation with Chris. This time I urged him to incorporate some of what he had learned about Chris's perspective into the discussion. The new conversation went like this:

Sam: Chris, I want to talk to you about how we work together. I know we have different work styles, and I want to find a way to collaborate so that we will both be happy.

Chris: Sam, I know you like to plan everything in advance, but I always get things done on time. I prefer to wait until I know exactly what the client wants before I invest too much effort. Overplanning is a waste of time. Besides, I have other things that I could be doing instead.

Sam: I understand where you are coming from. You like to be flexible, and I like to plan. I'm not saying you are wrong, although I like my way better, I'm just saying we need to find a way that works for both of us. I'm not trying to force you to do it my way; at the same time, I don't want to be forced to do it your way. How can we compromise?

Chris: I'd be willing to compromise. What do you suggest?

This conversation is far more constructive and much more likely to lead to resolution and compromise.

GUIDE TO THE PERPLEXED: FINDING THEIR STORY

So far we've seen that telling the other person's story is not as easy as it seems. Before we can begin to tell the other's story, we have to stop trying to be right. In addition, to tell the story accurately (i.e., as the other person would), we have to overcome nested unawareness—that is, we have to assume *we don't already know* the person's story. We need to cultivate a stance of uncertainty about what the other side actually thinks.

Sometimes, that's enough to get you over the finish line. Just putting yourself in the other person's shoes, even briefly, can immediately make his story clear. In Sam's case, once he let go of being right and looked at things through Chris's eyes, he was easily able to understand how Chris must feel and to tell Chris's story in a nuanced way. And getting help—from a colleague, a friend, your spouse, a manager—makes it easier as well.

But what if you still can't see how your counterparties see it? What can you do when you are clueless as to their story? What can you do when you are truly stuck? Here are three suggestions:

1. *Put the other person at the center of the narrative.* This means orienting the story toward whatever matters most to the other person, whatever issues most bother her, or whatever problems she suffers from. Why? Because that is how the other person experiences the situation. Consider my interaction with Evan, as described previously. In my story, Evan is a coworker who avoids conversation about difficult topics, making it difficult for us to work together. But if I put Evan at the center of the narrative, other details become important. For example, Evan may be thinking, "My manager is pressuring me into having a conversation that I'm not ready for. But I can't really say what I am thinking, because he is my boss, after all. He may act as if there is no power imbalance between us, but there is, because he pays my salary and can fire me. If I am honest and tell him I feel pressured into conversations, he might hold it against me and it could harm my career." When I tell the story this way, with Evan at the center, suddenly I realize that, for Evan, the hierarchy between us matters and dramatically affects the dynamic. That's a detail that simply didn't register when I put myself in the center, because it's not something that mattered to me.

2. *Make the other person the hero.* People tend to see themselves as good and as doing the right thing. Thus, in order to find their story, assume that they are playing a virtuous role in that story. In the interaction with Mina, the IT colleague in India, a helpful assumption is that Mina is somehow trying, in her own way, to do the right thing. This pushes us to explore how Mina's avoidance of a direct answer to her American counterpart's request might somehow be seen by her not as laziness

or an evasion, but as a constructive response. The cultural context in this case makes it clear how her behavior was an attempt to manage the situation as best as she could.

In the case of Tom, the Israeli who attended the dinner party, the host might consider how Tom may see himself as a scintillating dinner guest, not a rude one. And in the case of the two coworkers, Mary and Penelope, Penelope might consider that Mary is not being nosy, she is simply asking questions out of genuine fondness and concern.

3. *Make yourself the villain.* When we tell other people's stories, we have to realize that we are a part of their narrative, only not in the starring role we play in our own story. Quite the opposite—we are a supporting character while they are playing the lead. And in their narrative, they play a virtuous role, leaving us the opposite place in the dynamic. While the other person is the hero who is trying to save the day, you are the villain who in some way is up to no good and must be fought and resisted. Particularly when there is conflict, the other person's story assigns us a negative role and attributes nefarious motives for our behavior.

The interaction between Chris and Sam provides a vivid example. At the outset, Sam placed himself as the hero in his story—he was trying to make sure that the work got done on time and that the entire team could work together efficiently. In Sam's narrative, Chris was the villain, the selfish and lazy procrastinator who only cared about his own convenience. In order for Sam to understand Chris's story, he needed to reverse the roles. He needed to look for a story that would make *Chris* the hero and *Sam* the villain. By telling the story such that Sam was the villain, Sam realized (with some help) that for Chris, Sam was the pushy, bossy, controlling colleague who forced everyone else to work at his pace, and Chris was simply an efficient worker who didn't want to overplan and could better use his time on other projects, ultimately helping the company, rather than hurting it.

Uncomfortable though this last step may be, it is a powerful method of finding the other person's story. I believe that this method is especially difficult because it is so personal. To look at ourselves as the villain is unsettling and something most people resist. We must tell a story about ourselves that we not only feel is inaccurate, but from which we recoil. Sam knows he is not trying to be a bullying or controlling colleague, so when he is confronted with the possibility that Chris may think of him that way, his initial reaction is to protest that it is not true. It can be hurtful or frustrating for Sam to acknowledge that he may be seen that way by Chris. Nevertheless, by taking the extreme step of seeing himself as the villain, Sam understands Chris's story, and therefore he is in a much better position to engage with Chris and to have a constructive conversation.

HAVING THE CONVERSATION

Once you have truly told the other side's story, by putting the other person at the center and telling the narrative with a reverse-bias in which you play the villain, you are ready to engage with the other side.

Sometimes gaining an understanding of the other side's story can make a conversation unnecessary. Telling the other side's story can lead to a true moment of insight, completely changing your own frame of mind. Once Penelope understands that personal questions are Mary's way of showing caring and drawing closer and aren't meant to be intrusive, she might feel different about their office interaction. Having reframed Mary's behavior, she might no longer be offended. And that might make a conversation about their dynamic superfluous. Alternatively, she may feel less upset but still want to engage Mary and share how these questions make her feel awkward. And, feelings aside,

Penelope is still free to decline to answer questions that make her uncomfortable.

Nevertheless, in many or even most "stuck" situations, an honest and open conversation is still warranted. How can one build on the insights gained by telling the other person's story to foster constructive dialogue with the other side?

To begin, *acknowledge that the other side has a unique point of view,* which is as compelling to your counterpart as your own viewpoint is to you. This recognition sends a strong message of respect. It communicates that you view the other person as an equal, and that while you may not agree, you see her and her viewpoint as worthy of consideration. To begin a conversation with my colleague Evan, I might open by saying, "I'd like to talk about how we can best communicate, and I realize we may have different styles and preferences when it comes to having tough conversations."

Next, *describe their story before sharing your own.* It is tempting to begin by presenting your own story, but the more prudent path is to first summarize the other side's point of view. Why? When you summarize the other side's point of view, you achieve two things simultaneously.

First, you are verifying that you did indeed tell the other side's story accurately. If you got it right, you can then move forward in the conversation. If you misunderstood, the other side will correct you. That correction will allow you to glimpse for the first time how someone else sees the situation. Either way, you avoid proceeding based on a misunderstanding of the other side's perspective.

Second, summarizing the other side's perspective demonstrates that you understand them. People who feel understood are more likely to be open to your viewpoint than people who feel misunderstood. People who believe they are misunderstood will be constantly looking for an opportunity to show you their viewpoint, rather than listening to yours. Conversely, once you have shown that you truly understood their viewpoint, they are far more likely to listen to yours.

Thus, you might start your summary by saying, "I've thought about how you might be seeing things, and I would like to share with you what I came up with. Please let me know if I have understood you accurately, or if there are any key points that I missed."

Once you have summarized the other person's point of view accurately and gotten confirmation from the other side that he feels understood, you can *share your own viewpoint*. Here, it is important to consistently communicate that your goal is to share your own perspective with the other side, not to defeat the person or erase his point of view. Remind the other side that diversity of perspectives is natural, and you understand that other people have their own reasons for thinking as they do, just as you have your reasons for thinking as you do.

You might transition to sharing your own viewpoint by saying, "I want to share how I see things and also hear your reaction. I know we see this situation differently, which is normal, and my hope is that I can gain a better understanding of your view, and also have you learn more about how I see things. My goal is not to be 'right' in this conversation, but to understand and be understood."

Finally, as the conversation progresses, it is useful to *toggle between the different perspectives*. That is, intersperse a discussion of your own perspective with an acknowledgment of the other side's point of view. An example of toggling would be if Sam were to say to Chris, "I am frustrated when things are done at the last minute because it creates stress for me. At the same time, I understand that is how you work best." Or if Penelope were to say, "Mary, I get that the questions you ask about my personal life are your way of getting close and showing interest. At the same time, they make me very uncomfortable." The verbal pairing of both views—side by side, on equal footing—

reinforces your overall message that you are open to their point of view even though you may disagree.

By framing the dialogue as an opportunity to mutually share perspectives, rather than as a win-lose, zero-sum game, where one person's perspective must triumph over the other, you reduce defensiveness and increase openness. That, in turn, will lead to improved relationships and superior problem solving.

SEEING ISN'T (NECESSARILY) BELIEVING

The advice in this chapter may be difficult to swallow. You may be thinking, "What about my story? Why must I make myself the villain in order to have a conversation? And why am I the only one who has to stretch—shouldn't they be trying to tell my story also?"

If you are getting extremely frustrated, here is something to keep in mind: The goal of telling the other person's story, which requires reversing the bias in the other person's favor, is simply to *find* the person's story, not to agree with it. Just because Sam is able to tell a story where Chris is the hero, and even share with Chris that he understands that Chris feels a certain way, that doesn't make Chris right. Just because I can see that Evan is intimidated by me as his boss doesn't mean that I am trying to intimidate him. Telling a story where I am a villain does not make me an *actual* villain. Nor does it turn the other person into an actual hero. Indeed, often the other person's story is replete with rationalizations and other psychological defense mechanisms, and it may even contain elements that are objectively, verifiably untrue. Chris may, in fact, be a procrastinator who is self-centered. But identifying the person's story unlocks our ability to effectively engage with the other side. It gets us on the same page with the other person, putting us in a much better position to have a constructive conversation. And in that conversation, we are free to not only understand and empathize with the person's story, but also to share our own. We are free to push back and to disagree with what others say, but seeing their story first will make us more skillful in doing so, and it will make them more receptive to hearing us.

SUMMARY

One powerful way to flex your mind is to tell the other side's story as that person would tell it himself. This is surprisingly difficult to do in a stuck situation, when people tend to be unaware of the other side's story; moreover, they are "unaware that they are unaware."

To combat this situation, you need to truly put yourself in the other person's shoes. You need to strive to tell people's stories as they would themselves by putting them in the center, making them the hero, and making yourself the villain. This doesn't mean their stories are true or correct; nevertheless, suspending judgment and striving to tell their stories will help you flex your mind, paving the way to getting unstuck.

This chapter has focused on the other side's story, the flaws we are acutely aware of. However, just as they may be telling a story that is not completely accurate, we are likely doing the same. While Chris may be a procrastinator, Sam might also be a bit controlling and pushy. In many cases, *our* story, with its blind spots and biases, is part of the problem. Learning to see ourselves and our story from the outside is the subject of the next chapter.

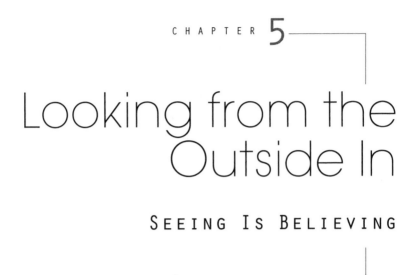

CHAPTER 5

Looking from the Outside In

SEEING IS BELIEVING

Albert, a brilliant scientist leading a team engaged in cutting-edge research, was struggling to accept the feedback I had shared with him. "I don't think I am intimidating at all. I have no problem when people disagree with me. I welcome contrary points of view. I never raise my voice or insult people that work in my lab, although I got plenty of that when I was a newly minted Ph.D. The problem is with the team. They need to show more initiative."

A few weeks before, Albert had called me asking for help. He said that the provost of the research university where he worked wanted him to get coaching to work on his management skills. Albert acknowledged that there was a problem, but he didn't know how to solve it. After meeting with Albert, I arranged a series of interviews with his entire research staff, asking for their candid feedback on Albert. Nearly everyone said that the reason people did not push back on Albert was that he was intimidating. He would rip people's ideas to shreds. True, they said, he rarely if ever yelled. But he could be extremely sarcastic, embarrassing his research assistants in front of others. Moreover, he only gave negative feedback, never praise or acknowledgment of a job well done. The result: People felt intimidated by him.

Yet when I shared this feedback with Albert, he resisted, claiming it was inaccurate. Instead, he shifted the burden onto his team. I pushed back on Albert, saying, "Let's look at what people said about you. You rip people's ideas to pieces to uncover flaws in their thinking. You are sarcastic and embarrass people in front of their peers. And you rarely give positive feedback. If you were your own boss, wouldn't that be pretty intimidating?"

It's difficult to imagine the way that we are perceived by others. But getting an outside point of view on how others experience us is essential for creating a flexible mind. This chapter will help you with the challenging task of seeing yourself from the outside in, so that you are more aware of the impact that you have on those around you. Being more aware of yourself allows you to make unilateral changes that can unlock your stuck situations.

WHAT DO I SOUND LIKE FROM THE OUTSIDE?

Have you ever heard your own voice on a recording? I am willing to bet your first reaction was, "Wow, I don't really sound like that, do I?" You might even have denied that the recording was accurate. "My voice isn't actually that nasal, is it?" "I don't really mumble that badly." "Do I always talk so quickly?" It is a natural reaction. I have been using voice mail for decades. Nevertheless, whenever I first record my outgoing message on a new voice mail system, it takes me a few tries before I'm able to accept that my voice sounds like me.

Naturally, it's completely misguided for me to insist, "That isn't how I sound." Of course that is how I sound—to everyone else in the world. That's because the recording is an accurate replication of how I sound on the *outside*. It is how everyone else is used to hearing me—from the outside. I, on the other hand, am used to hearing myself from the *inside*. The difference is subtle, but it's more than enough to make me deny that my "outside" voice is how I really sound. But of course, deep down, I know that it is.

This physical metaphor has profound relevance for our topic. In Chapter Four, we talked about how to tune into the other side's story. Here, we are going to learn how to tune into ourselves and our role in the situation. That is, we are going to examine our own behavior and its impact. But in this case, we are going to look at ourselves through the "objective" lens of an outsider.

Like the voice on the answering machine, the way we think we come across can be quite different from how we actually come across to others. And the gap tends to be biggest in our stuck situations. Our lack of self-awareness is greatest in those situations that give us the most trouble.

Consider the following example: Joy, a participant in one of my workshops, had been struggling with her new role as a team leader for software development.[1] Joy described her difficulties with one team member in particular, a man named Hank. Although a talented contributor to the team, Hank was consistently late in completing his work. His tardiness ended up affecting other team members' progress, and frequently Joy would simply do Hank's work herself, just to keep the project moving forward. She was frustrated with his behavior but unsure of what to do.

When I asked what happened when she raised the topic with Hank, Joy said that he would minimize the problem and blithely promise to be more punctual in the future. Hank had made this commitment several times, Joy said, but nothing had changed.

Then I asked Joy if we could role-play her conversation with Hank. The conversation went like this:

Joy: Hank, I need to talk to you.

Me (as Hank): Okay, what's up?

Joy: Do you know when you will have your project assignment completed?

Me (as Hank): Yeah, it's almost done. I'll try to get it to you next week.

Joy: Okay. That would be great.

Me: (as Hank): Sure, no problem.

I invited Joy to try being more direct with Hank about her frustration and the impact his tardiness was having on her and the team. We role-played again:

Joy: Hank, it would be great if you could finish the project assignment as soon as possible.

Me (as Hank): No problem. But you know how overloaded I am.

Joy: Yes, I understand that. Still, it's very important, so please try to get to it when you are able. . . .

Me (as Hank): Will do.

I asked Joy if she felt she was being direct, and she said yes. I then asked the group who had been observing the role play if they thought she was being direct, and they all said no. I pointed out that Hank (as played by me) definitely was not "getting" how frustrated she was.

I asked Joy to have the conversation once more, only this time she should try an "overshoot." The goal of an overshoot is to stretch one's muscles. I didn't want Joy to practice communicating in a realistic way, but to be as assertive and direct as possible. She should feel free to yell, get angry, use profanity—anything that would communicate her frustration with Hank. Indeed, Joy should exaggerate her behavior in this role play and strive to go beyond what would be permissible or constructive in real life.

Joy's *overshoot* conversation went like this:

Joy: Hank, I need to talk to you.

Me (as Hank): Okay, what's up?

Joy: Do you know when you will have the project assignment ready?

Me (as Hank): Yeah, it's almost done. I'll try to get it to you next week.

Joy: Hank, I really need your work. It's holding everyone else back, and it wastes a lot of time when you are late.

Me (as Hank): I'm sorry, but I'm overloaded.

Joy: Well, this needs to get done, because it's urgent. I know you have other things on your plate, but you made a commitment to me and to the team. Maybe we should have someone else assigned to the team to take your place if you are too busy.

Me (as Hank): No, I want to be on the team. I'll get right on it.

Joy: Can we agree to a specific date? Can you have it done by this Friday?

Me (as Hank): Yeah, it's almost done. I will make sure to have it by Friday.

Joy: Thank you.

How did Joy feel about her overshoot conversation? She said it made her uncomfortable, and she felt being so direct was rude. Then I then turned to the others in the group and asked for their input. Every one of them said that Joy's conversation was entirely appropriate and professional and not at all extreme. From my perspective, playing the role of Hank, I did not experience the conversation as rude or overly aggressive, either. In fact, it was quite possible that Hank wasn't even aware of Joy's frustration or the impact his lateness was having on the team because they had never had such a direct conversation.

What is striking about Joy's situation was the gap between how she perceived herself and how everyone else perceived her. Joy thought that she was being direct with Hank and sharing her frustrations with him, when in reality she was quite timid and indirect. And when urged to exaggerate and behave as assertively as possible, Joy produced a dialogue that was firm yet polite, and certainly not inappropriate. And yet, in that conversation, Joy still saw herself as stepping over the line of appropriateness.

Joy was failing to see herself from the outside in. Helping her get unstuck in her interactions with Hank required helping her flex her mind to see herself as others saw her.

At stake for Joy is more than just her stuck dynamic with Hank. Joy's struggles with assertiveness are almost certainly a part of her stuck situations with other people as well. For most of us, our weaknesses, flaws, and blind spots are quite consistent, so working on these weaknesses can yield long-lasting benefits by having a positive effect on most of our difficult interactions.

SIMPLE, BUT NOT EASY

It would seem that seeing oneself from the outside should be pretty easy. It's as simple as getting feedback from other people, having them tell you how you come across to them, and then adjusting your behavior accordingly. Easy, right?

Well, not so fast. People often resist seeing themselves from the outside. It's threatening, because it requires that they change their perspective and their perception of themselves. Albert, for example, had a clear picture in his mind of what it means to be intimidating. Intimidating people yell, scream, and threaten—and he did none of those things. Albert failed to see was how his difficult questions, sarcastic tone, and negative feedback were indeed intimidating to many people. Naturally, Albert wasn't trying to intimidate anyone. But that is the effect he was having.

For Albert to accept that people experienced him as intimidating and learn to change his behavior, he would need to suspend his own disbelief. He would have to let go of his own self-perception and concede that someone else might be better at telling him how he comes across than he is himself. He would have to be willing to defer to another point of view, but on a very personal topic: himself.

To Albert's credit, he was open to this feedback (more so than other clients I've worked with). Although he resisted at first, he recognized that in order to unlock his "stuck" situation with his employees, he had no choice but to flex his mind and look at himself from the outside in.

Now let's consider another example: Bob was a fabulous technologist. He had a deep and precise knowledge of complex systems. He was creative. And he was fast. Bob devised innovative solutions to client's technical problems, saving both time and money. If Bob could so effectively solve complex problems, what was the problem?

The problem was that Bob was a jerk. He told one nervous client, "Your issue is not a crisis. If you would quit asking me about it, I could get to it sooner. Don't call me about this again." He was abusive to coworkers, telling one employee, "Your question is not only stupid, it's also something I answered yesterday. Why are you wasting my time?" His acerbic comments, abrasive manner, and harsh sense of "humor" succeeded in annoying nearly everyone around him. Bob's raw talent and technical expertise had, so far, allowed him to succeed as a technology team leader, despite his lack of interpersonal skills. But with the economy mired in a recession, being smart wasn't enough. Bob was failing to retain clients. Bob's manager hired me to coach Bob, saying he needed to improve.

Everyone knew Bob needed to change, except for Bob. When I shared the feedback I had collected about him from clients, peers, direct reports, and others, Bob quickly said, "It's not my fault that people are oversensitive." When I cited specific examples, he said, "Oh, it's not that bad. People are making a big deal over nothing." My attempts to coach Bob on his communication style failed because Bob was locked into his own way of thinking. He simply couldn't, or wouldn't, flex his mind to see himself as other's saw him. He kept insisting, "That's not me." Until Bob changed his thinking, he could not solve his problem.

Turning to technology for help, I set up a video camera and recorded Bob interacting with me as I variously played the roles of one of his clients, one of his colleagues, and one of his direct reports. Then I stopped the recording and asked Bob to watch himself on video.

The effect was powerful. For the first time perhaps in his life, Bob stepped outside of the conversation and looked at himself from the outside in. With his own eyes, he was able to see how his behavior was causing the jarring conversations and negative feedback. Once Bob changed his thinking by incorporating how others saw him, he was ready to work on how to change his communication.

DEALING WITH DENIAL

Everyone resists the kind of feedback that Albert, Joy, and Bob received. It is unnerving, even shocking, to discover a big gap between how we sound from the inside vs. the outside. But most people are able to take in the feedback when confronted with the supporting data. In Albert's case, it was the interviews I conducted with his staff members; in Joy's case, it was the workshop setting and the impressions of everyone in the room; and in Bob's case, it was a videotape of himself that provided the evidence. They each accepted the feedback and were willing to work to change their behavior.

However, people can be tenacious when it comes to their psychological defense mechanisms, such that they protect themselves even when faced with overwhelming data. I have encountered a few clients who were extremely resistant to change, with defenses that kept them safely insulated from feedback.

Stan was a doctor who headed up a large division of a hospital. While everyone recognized how bright he was and applauded his tremendous accomplishments, it was also universally recognized that Stan was difficult to work with. I was asked to coach Stan to help him improve his relationships with staff members.

I conducted a series of interviews with Stan's colleagues, some who liked him and some who hated him, asking for honest feedback. Everyone said the same thing: Stan was a difficult person. He would yell at people, interrupt them, embarrass his staff in front of other people, and so on. Phrases such as "the single most difficult person I have ever worked for in my career" were used more than once.

After collecting comments from the various interviews in a written report, I shared the findings with Stan. I was nervous about doing so, since they were such shockingly brutal comments. Indeed, I was embarrassed on Stan's behalf just listening to the feedback and writing it down and feared that hearing all of this would crush Stan. Nevertheless, I scheduled a meeting with Stan and told him what everyone said about him.

The good news is that Stan was not crushed. The not-so-good news is that Stan did not seem to care, because he rejected the feedback entirely. He defended himself, saying, "Many of the people there are frustrated because I pushed them to work harder, and so behind my back they bad-mouth me," and "I am not really that difficult to deal with," and "This hospital is full of corruption and waste; this was the only way to get things done."

I was completely taken aback by Stan's ability to block out concrete data. Every one of the interviewees said the same things about him, using almost identical language. Yet Stan brushed it all off, insisting that the feedback was simply untrue. How was this possible?

In a word, the answer is denial. Seeing one's self-image contradicted is painful, sometimes too painful to bear. So people deny the feedback and cling to their existing self-image.

In one sense, Stan is an outlier, since his story is extreme in how forcefully and unanimously his coworkers, even those who admired him, described their difficulties in working with him. But it would be a mistake to see Stan as a monster or a jerk. He was a highly principled individual, deeply committed to his patients. And he believed in what he was doing. In that sense, Stan is very much the norm.

Consider this: Can you see any part of yourself in Stan? That is, have you ever fought and fought against feedback about yourself, only to realize, perhaps years later, that the feedback was true and that you should accept it? It's much easier to recognize when other people are in denial about themselves; seeing our own blindness is orders of magnitude more difficult.

Stan's story has relevance for all of us, being an extreme version of the psychological defense mechanisms we all employ. Thus, it's worth examining the mechanics of how Stan rejected his feedback, so we can avoid making the same mistake. He made two arguments, which will be dealt with in turn.

First, Stan insisted that the situation was more complex than people were giving him credit for. He explained that he was often extremely patient and tolerant of people's shortcomings. He was willing to invest in training his people to help them get promoted. He said that whenever he had to crack the whip to get something done, it was because the stakes were high, patients were at risk, and the cost of letting things slide was too great. Moreover, many of the people who complained were low performers, who resented the higher standards he held them to, and thus they had a reason to put down Stan behind his back.

Stan's point has merit. Remember the example I gave of listening to your own voice on a recording? It's useful but simplistic: Recording technology is highly accurate, and I have little choice but to accept that I sound different to others than I do to myself. But real-life stuck situations are multifaceted. Stan did invest in training people, and he did hold staff to a higher standard than had been the case before. Undoubtedly there was resentment toward him because he made people work harder. And the stakes were high, with patient care hanging in the balance.

At the same time, this is a powerful defense mechanism precisely because it is always true. Situations *are* complex. There *are* multiple factors involved in any stuck interaction. When confronted with difficult feedback, it's always tempting to go down this road and say, "Well, you have to understand things are not that simple . . ." Frequently, complexity is used to minimize one's own shortcomings and show how other people or the situation are making things get stuck. The "complexity defense" can never be refuted completely, and a person who truly does not want to look from the outside in can always take refuge in complexity. Stan certainly tried to.

In reality, this line of thinking avoids the really important question, which is: Does this feedback offer you a perspective that can help you improve your stuck situation? If so, embrace it. Don't hide from your own learning the way Stan did. Even if the situation is more complex than the feedback about you suggests, use it as an opportunity to change and grow.

Stan's second line of defense was that while his style may have been harsh, it was the only way to get things done. In his words, "Because of the deep inefficiencies and inadequate level of patient care I encountered when I got here, the only way to make a change was through brutal honesty and a tough, uncompromising approach to managing staff. I was hired to get results, which is what I did."

We all have a little bit of Stan inside us. We all justify some of our flaws by saying they were essential to our success. Marshall Goldsmith, the well-known author and executive coach, writes persuasively on this topic in his book *What Got You Here Won't Get You There.*[2] People take vices—such as a tendency to humiliate staff members—and turn them into virtues, claiming they are unavoidable and even indispensable to achieving results.

For Stan, and for all of us, learning new and better ways to interact with others requires letting go of old and often destructive ways of doing things. Just because something worked in the past doesn't mean it's the best way. Your past success doesn't magically ennoble anything and everything you did along the way to get there. It doesn't transform every character flaw into a deep source of strength. Sometimes you succeeded *despite* those very factors you thought were helping you. So a person needs to come at this topic with a mind open to hearing, "Maybe my old way wasn't the best way. And maybe I'm coming across differently to other people—different from how I think I am."

Stan, like all of us, can't learn something new until he accepts that there may be a better way to do things. This is hard, because the old way *feels* so right. Being polite to an extreme feels right to Joy—but that doesn't mean it is the best way to interact with her coworker. We all need to cultivate openness to new ways of doing things, but first we need openness to seeing that our old way isn't the best or only way, and it might actually be pretty bad.

IT'S NOT YOU, IT'S ME

There is a funny episode of the television program *Seinfeld* where George's girlfriend is breaking up with him, and in an attempt to let him down easy, she says, "It's not you, it's me." George, being familiar with this technique for dumping someone, rejects the line, saying, "No one says, 'It's not you, it's me,' to me. If it's anyone, it's me!" And his girlfriend finally admits, "All right, it's you!"[3]

The scene works because people know that when you don't want to hurt someone's feelings, you lie, and say the problem is not the other person. The scene also works because deep down, we rarely believe the problem truly is us. As George's girlfriend admits, the problem really is George.

The writers of *Seinfeld* created a funny skit built on a fundamental truth—people look at a situation and naturally see why the other person is at fault. People don't see their own flaws, or if they do, they minimize their importance. Put another way, whenever things go wrong, we all tend to secretly believe "it's not me, it's you!" And so, looking from the outside in requires us to reverse that bias and always ask, "How might it be me, after all?"

In my work with clients over the years, this is often the point where they raise the question that was first discussed in Chapter One. They say to me, "Why are you making this all my fault? Isn't the other side also accountable? Why do other people get a free pass?"

It's an important question. Even if Albert is intimidating—aren't his employees on the hook for confronting him when they disagree? Even if Bob is abrasive—aren't the clients accountable for making unreasonable demands? Even if Stan is difficult and demanding—shouldn't the hospital staff be held responsible for delivering adequate patient care?

Here's the point: The other side does not get a free pass. Other people *are* also on the hook. But the most leverage that we have to change a dynamic comes from changing ourselves. By behaving differently, we can influence the other person's behavior. The point is not to score each side and determine whose conduct is worse; it's to make things go better. And in fact, finding out that I am part of the problem is not bad news, it is good news! It's good news because it means that I can do something about it. Notwithstanding our natural tendency to try to show why we are not at fault, it's much better to find out how we *are* at fault so that we know what to work on. How much more troubling would it be if Stan, for example, had been a terrific manager but was simply bad-mouthed by lazy and vindictive staff members who leveled unjustified criticism? He couldn't do much to change that, aside from finding a new job.

Keep this in mind: Finding out that "It's not you, it's me" is a *good* thing. We need to fight our biases, resist that defensive urge, and ask, "What am I doing that is making this situation go badly? How can I better see myself from the outside in?"

LEARNING ABOUT MYSELF— GOING DEEP

Looking from the outside in provides another wonderful opportunity, which is for deeper self-awareness. It's not just a chance to learn about my behavior; it's a chance for me to understand better what makes me tick. The insights I glean can help me learn what I need to do to succeed, what types of jobs or personalities I work with best, and what I most need to look for in a partner or subordinate to compensate for my weaknesses.

A good friend was purchasing a summer home and wanted

advice on how to negotiate with the seller. I was happy to help and worked with my friend to help him think through his options. We got deep into the details of the negotiation, including price, financial terms, and timing of the closing. After we had been talking for about thirty minutes, my friend's wife joined the conversation and said, "I want you to keep this private. Please don't share the fact that we're purchasing a summer home with anyone—not even your wife."

Although I didn't react, I found her comment upsetting and even insulting. Of course I would keep their confidence and not share what we discussed with other people. But my wife is in a different category. It is understood that spouses share everything—the foundation of a marriage is trust and openness, and to ask someone to keep a secret from his spouse undermines that foundation. How could my friend's wife even suggest that I would keep something from my wife—especially when I was doing them the favor by helping them with their negotiation?

Later I discussed this request for secrecy with my wife (as I said, we don't have secrets), telling her how disturbed I was, confident that she would back me up and share my sense of outrage. To my surprise, she said, "I think you are overreacting."

I was flabbergasted. How could my own wife, with whom I share a marriage and a deep commitment to not keep anything from each other, not share my feelings of outrage?

My wife continued: "You are taking this too personally. I'm not saying you had to agree to her request to keep the matter a secret from me, but you have to keep in mind that not everyone has the same attitude toward marriage. Many couples share some things and keep other things separate. Someone else might have said to her, 'No problem.' I think the more interesting question is this: Why are you getting so upset?"

My wife's comment stopped me in my tracks. I paused and considered the situation, and I realized that she was right.

You see, while I tend to be somewhat private, within my

closest relationships I am quite open. I don't like to keep things secret, even if it leads to challenging or painful conversations. I prefer to raise even difficult topics with my close family members and friends. And this is certainly true about my relationship with my wife—I don't keep secrets, and even suggesting that I would goes against my grain. That's just how I am.

Of course, not everyone is like me. Not everyone is comfortable sharing everything, or wants to share everything, even in close relationships, such as with one's spouse. There are many different models for a successful marriage. Naturally, my way—sharing everything and keeping no secrets from my spouse—feels right to me. I might even recommend it to other people as the secret to a happy marriage. But I shouldn't judge my friends' request through the lens of my own tendencies. They may have a different kind of marriage, one where this request would be the most normal thing imaginable.

Thus, I learned something important from this entire exchange—not about marriage, but about myself. I learned that because openness and honesty in relationships is extremely important to me, maybe more so than to most people, I am quite invested in defending my way of doing things. I am also likely to react strongly whenever it comes up. You might even say it's one of my "hot buttons."

What's the benefit of becoming aware of my hot buttons? Why does it matter? It matters because unless I can recognize my hot-button issue, I won't be able to assess this exchange in an objective way. And this isn't true for just this one situation. Anytime I confront a similar situation—a relationship where I feel someone is not being open or honest with me, or when someone accuses me of not being open with her—I am liable to react intensely. It's not that my reaction is wrong or illegitimate. Rather, when I flex my mind and look at this exchange from the outside in, I can see that my reaction is subjective. In this example, my outrage at my friend's request says much more about *me* than it does about the request itself. That is the essence of looking at yourself from the outside in.

Many stuck situations at work have within them deep truths about who we are and how we get stuck; tackling these types of situations can lead to powerful insights.

I once coached a midlevel executive named Frances. Frances was bright, hardworking, and highly valued by her manager, a senior executive at the company. Indeed, she was a rising star. However, Frances's direct reports found her difficult to work with. They complained to her manager that Frances gave them almost no guidance on how to approach their assignments. She also had unrealistic expectations on how quickly they should be able to finish a difficult assignment. Finally, they did not feel inspired working for Frances. She never gave them positive feedback or showed appreciation for their efforts. All in all, they found working with her to be pretty miserable. It was at this point that I was asked to coach Frances one-on-one to help her become a better manager.

I began the coaching process by asking Frances a series of questions to learn about her work style and preferences. Three findings in particular gave me insight into Frances.

First of all, Frances told me she was extremely hardworking. She would periodically work in the office until midnight or later when necessary to complete an assignment.

Second, Frances was a self-starter who was most comfortable working without a lot of guidance. Indeed, she much preferred managers who delegated tasks and let her decide how to approach them, rather than micromanaging and spoon-feeding her every detail. When she encountered problems, she preferred to solve them on her own, rather than ask for help.

Finally, while Frances was tenacious in how she approached her work, she was modest, even self-conscious, about her accomplishments. She avoided the spotlight and became embarrassed when she was singled out for praise on a successful assignment. She hated it when one of the senior executives would publicly thank her for her hard work while on a group conference call. It made her uncomfortable, but she had no choice but to suffer through it.

Naturally, these insights into Frances's style helped me make sense of her perspective on her relationship with her direct reports. They helped me understand her story.

When I shared with Frances the feedback given by her direct reports, I asked her what she thought about their comments. In reply, she said, "I think the analysts are immature. When I was an analyst, I hardly got any guidance at all, and I would put in long hours figuring things out on my own before I ran to my manager to explain it to me. And to be honest, I find it absurd that I am working until midnight or later and these analysts are going home at 7:00 or 8:00 p.m. They are lazy." When I specifically asked about giving credit to her team and showing appreciation for their work, she said, "I think that's ridiculous. People shouldn't need to get 'credit' for doing their job. It's not something that I am comfortable getting or giving. I just don't think it's appropriate. This whining attitude is hard for me to take."

At this point it became clear that there was a large gap between Frances and her direct reports on at least three concrete questions:

- How many hours should employees spend at work each day?
- How much guidance should a direct report receive when being given an assignment?
- How much verbal appreciation should managers give their employees?

There may or may not be objectively "correct" answers to these questions; more than likely the answers would depend almost entirely on the context. But looking for answers would have been a mistake. The problem here was primarily one of communication about expectations. Frances and her direct reports needed to find a way to discuss their expectations with one another and negotiate a constructive working relationship.

Hearing Frances talk about her direct reports and what she thought of their requests for guidance and appreciation made it clear how *her own biases* were preventing her from having clear, constructive conversations and good working relationships with them.

Frances was an extremely hard worker, perhaps even a workaholic, so she saw anyone who did not work as hard as she did, or in the way she did, as lazy. She struggled to see legitimacy in balancing work and personal life in a way that was different from her own.

Frances craved autonomy and independence, so she viewed her direct reports' need for guidance as a form of immaturity or lack of initiative. She failed to see that, while individuals' styles may vary, a request for reasonable guidance was normal, and it was her job as a manager to provide that guidance. Frances was limited to seeing the situation through the lens of her own style.

Frances was uncomfortable getting or giving recognition, which blinded her to other people's needs. This was perhaps the most striking example of how Frances was a prisoner of her biases. Most people would value being given credit for their work; at the very least, they would not loathe being verbally appreciated by their manager. Because of Frances's aversion to being on the receiving end of a public thank-you, she could not imagine a desire for appreciation being legitimate, instead labeling her direct reports "whiners."

In this case, looking from the outside in required Frances to consider how her own experience and attitudes contributed to the dynamic between her and her subordinates. Frances needed to understand and identify the particular traits that marked her work as an individual contributor, and later as a manager.

Frances liked independence and the challenge of working hard, and she preferred to work anonymously, without recognition. If Frances were able to identify these traits in herself, it would be easier for her to see that not every employee was like her. Indeed, many or even most people would want a bit more guidance than Frances. Similarly, anonymity in one's work may not suit everyone.

This realization could allow her to see something that is even more difficult to accept. Perhaps her way is *not* the best way. While Frances was comfortable with minimal guidance from her managers, it may be inefficient to "reinvent the wheel" every time she encountered a problem. Perhaps Frances would have been able to accomplish just as much in less time, and avoid working until midnight so frequently, if she had occasionally asked for help. And maybe Frances's aversion to accepting praise is a problem. Her direct reports are typical in their desire for appreciation—it's a need that nearly everyone has, and wanting or needing to hear thanks once in a while is simply human nature. Frances's abhorrence of it is extreme, and will likely be an issue for her with nearly every direct report that she may encounter in her career.

LOOKING IN THE MIRROR

Diagnosing what was going on for Frances and seeing how her style and preferences were creating blind spots for her was only part of the battle. The next step was to help Frances see what I saw.

Before I could coach Frances on how to interact with her analysts differently, I needed her to understand how her approach was limiting her understanding of the situation. The message I needed to deliver was, "Frances, a big part of the problem is you." And I would need to deliver it with great care.

My conversation with Frances went as follows:

Me: What do you think of what your direct reports have said about working with you?

Frances: I think it's unfair. As I said, I think they are whiners and they are being coddled. I don't ask them to do anything that I have not already done and continue to do myself.

Me: Frances, before I say anything else, I want to acknowledge the tremendous success you've had at this company, and recognize that your work style has not only worked for you, but made you a valuable member of this team.

This last statement, which acknowledges Frances's point of view, is essential, because I am about to ask her to do something terribly uncomfortable. I am going to ask Frances to consider that her way is not universal, and that it may in fact be flawed. Thus, I need Frances to hear that I am not *rejecting* her point of view in favor of the view of her analysts. Rather, I want her to "get it" by considering her own view from the outside in. Having done that, Frances will be ready to engage with her analysts in a different way.

Frances: Thank you.

Me: Having said that, I want you to try to look at this from their point of view.

Frances: I understand their point of view. They want to be coddled.

Me: I hear them asking for more input from you on assignments. Do you think that is coddling?

Frances: Obviously, it's a judgment call on how much guidance to give an employee. If I have to give them so much guidance, they stop being autonomous employees and start to be just a pair of hands that type what I tell them to type. I want them to think on their own.

Me: I think your point about it being a judgment call is exactly right. And here's the thing: I think your tendency, your personal style, is to want and need minimal direction. Would you agree?

Frances: Yeah, I think that's fair.

Me: And I think you are judging your subordinates by the standard of what you would want if you were in their situation. Correct?

Frances: Probably.

Me: But Frances—they are not you. Not everyone likes to be given total freedom and autonomy to figure everything out for themselves.

Frances: Why not?

Me: Because people are really different from each other.

Frances: Don't you think they are being a little immature? Don't you think they should try to think for themselves?

Me: Here's how I see it, Frances. I do think people should try to think for themselves. And I am not saying they are all right and you are all wrong. I am saying that you are a bit extreme in your preference for almost zero guidance. And I think that your aversion to giving your employees more guidance says more about you and your tendencies than it does about whether their requests for guidance are reasonable.

Frances: Hmm.

Me: I want to take this point even further. You hate being thanked publicly. There's nothing wrong with that. But that's your thing. It's not an objective truth that thanking people publicly is wrong or unnecessary. It's unnecessary *for you*. But many, maybe even most people in the world are not like you. And you need to remember that, because if you try to apply the standard of your own preferences to everyone in the world on the issue of getting or giving public thanks, you will quickly realize that *you* are the outlier. You don't need to feel bad or apologize. You just need to recognize that when the issue of showing or receiving praise and appreciation comes up, there is a high likelihood that it is "your thing" playing out, not theirs.

Frances: So what are you suggesting?

Me: I'm suggesting that before you have a conversation with one of the people reporting to you, consider whether this might be your own blind spot. Because once you see that, I think your whole approach to the conversation will be different.

Frances: Hmm. I need to think about that.

This conversation needed to be handled with sensitivity and care. How do you tell someone that her internal barometer for assessing what is appropriate in this situation is off? There is no pain-free way to do it that I know of. But the best approach is to be empathetic and to send a clear message that you are *not* blaming the individual for the whole situation; rather, you are offering a framework that will allow the person to become more self-aware, and thus change the situation by changing her own expectations and behavior.

Subsequently I had another conversation with Frances. This time she told me that she had considered the feedback and decided there was merit in it. She recounted that when she was a junior staff member, she got along very well with a manager who most of her peers did not like. And in retrospect, what she liked was probably what most people disliked: This manager was known for giving little guidance, minimal feedback, and a ton of autonomy. Thus, her preferences in work style were already identifiable back then.

Frances also shared the fact that her discomfort with praise was largely a product of the culture she was raised in. Growing up, people rarely gave compliments, and any compliments that were paid were immediately deflected. To do otherwise was considered poor manners. Since Frances was aware that not everyone was raised in this style, it would be natural that other people would not find praise so uncomfortable.

I'd like to reiterate a point that I made earlier: Frances's discovery that a big part of the problem was herself was good news, not bad. This breakthrough doesn't let the analysts off the hook;

it just means that Frances can unilaterally change the situation just by changing her own perspective.

PRACTICING HOW TO LOOK FROM THE OUTSIDE IN

At this point, you may believe in the power of looking from the outside in. But the million-dollar question is: How do you do it? How do you see something that, by definition, is a blind spot?

There is no foolproof way. It's more art than science, and there is no formula to get you there. However, there are things you can do to make progress.

First, *begin by questioning yourself.* Make it a habit to always ask yourself, "How might I be coming across to the other person?" or "What am I doing to make this situation worse, or keep it from getting better?" This line of questioning is, of course, a reversal of the natural reaction, which is to always ask, "What is the other side doing wrong?" The simple fact of asking this question can help hone your awareness and sensitivity to your own behavior.

Second, *look for patterns.* You may notice similarities in the kinds of situations that tend to get you stuck. Joy, the software development team leader described previously in this chapter, had a challenge with Hank that related to her ability to be assertive. Joy might notice on her own that situations where she needs to be assertive and ask for things tend to give her trouble, suggesting a blind spot. Bob, the fabulous technologist, gets consistent feedback from many different sources saying that he has great technical expertise but abrasive interpersonal skills. That consistency suggests he may have an issue in this area.

Third, *watch for intense emotional reactions* to certain kinds of situations. Emotions may signal that you have a blind spot. The intensity of my feelings about being told not to openly share information with my wife was a clue that I needed to look inside myself. If I were to look at other relationships and situations where I reacted (or overreacted) to people I felt were not being completely open or honest, I might see a pattern emerge.

Finally, another strategy you can try is to *solicit help from others.* An outsider can often see and describe to you the things you are missing. Finding the right person or people to ask for help can be tricky, though. Because you are going to ask for help with a blind spot, you won't be fully able to judge the accuracy of the feedback; after all, the definition of a blind spot is that your vision there is limited. So it's important to get the right source.

A metaphor to think of is choosing a doctor. The minimal criterion is expertise. I need to find a doctor who is skilled, so graduating from a reputable medical school and having received good training are basic requirements. But in most big cities in the United States, there are many doctors who exceed that minimal threshold. Beyond that, intangible factors play an important role in choosing a doctor, and one of the most important intangibles is trust. Trust matters, because when it comes to medicine, I am not in a position to second-guess the doctor; I simply do not have the expertise. As a patient I am flying blind, in a sense, and I need to know I can trust that the doctor is doing a good job.

But trust matters on another level. I need to be open and honest with my doctor and be willing to both share difficult things about myself (e.g., my sexual history, my eating habits, symptoms I am having) and to hear difficult feedback about myself (e.g., how important it is that I lose weight, get tested for genetic diseases, change my lifestyle). If I don't trust my doctor, I may not go to her and/or I may not be open to hearing her advice.

And so soliciting feedback and help is a similar process: Choose someone that you trust to give you the outsider perspective. You will almost certainly become defensive, and a trusted source is the best person to handle your reaction and help you get past it.

It's useful to prime the person you are asking for help by explaining that what you want is not sympathy and cheerleading, but actual, honest feedback. You might say something like, "I don't want you to just agree with me and support me. I want you to tell me what you see *me* doing wrong here, so that I can learn and grow."

A professional coach can play this role. A coach who has both expertise and a relationship of trust with a client is ideal. The examples given in this chapter demonstrate how coaching can be powerful way of unlocking stuck situations.

In addition to hiring a coach, you can turn to the people you work with—your manager, a colleague, even a direct report. Many people I have spoken with use their significant other or close family members as trusted sources of feedback. The key is to identify people who know you and will be honest with you.

If you suspect that there is an area you need to work on, you can turn to technology. Listening to an audio recording or watching a video recording of yourself can provide an outsider's view (although a recording won't be an empathetic listener when you get defensive).

HAVING THE CONVERSATION

The hardest part of learning to see from the outside in is overcoming your own internal barriers. If you are able to do that, you are more than halfway there. The next step is talking about your own blind spots with the other side; this conversation has the potential to radically transform your interactions and help you get unstuck.

Here are a few pieces of advice on how to have a conversation that incorporates the insights you gleaned from looking from the outside in:

▷ *Acknowledge up front that your behavior has been part of the problem.* This does not necessarily mean taking sole responsibility for everything. It just means stating that you recognize you have a blind spot that has contributed to the negative dynamic.

▷ *Ask for the other person's input on how your behavior has come across.* This achieves two purposes simultaneously. First, it allows the other side a chance to air his feelings and also feel heard, which will almost certainly have a positive impact on the situation. Second, it gives you a chance to learn potentially new information that you may not already know about how you come across to others. After all, you may be trying to look from the outside in, but here you are getting feedback "hot off the press" and right from the horse's mouth, so to speak (forgive the mixed metaphors).

▷ *Summarize what you hear.* You want to show people that you've listened and absorbed their feedback. This further ensures that the other side feels heard.

▷ *Share your own reflections on what you want to try to do differently.* You may ask for other people's advice or help in improving on your blind spot. You might apologize for the unintended impact of your words. You should do what feels right in the context—but make sure to complete this part of the conversation before moving on to other topics and issues, such as engaging in problem solving and so on. Don't rush matters: It's worth going slow to make sure your message is understood. Consider that your counterpart may not even realize at first that you are trying to take responsibility for your own behavior.

Below is a conversation that Frances was able to have with one of her subordinates named Alan. They met one-on-one to talk through the issues, and I coached her on how to bring her newfound self-awareness into the conversation. Here is the dialogue:

Frances: Alan, I want to talk to you about how we can work together more effectively. I think my own biases and behaviors as a manager are probably part of why we are having trouble.

Alan: Okay.

Frances: First of all, I want you to know that your feedback is important to me, and I need to hear it so that I can improve as a manager.

Alan: I appreciate that.

Frances: Do you feel like you get enough guidance from me?

Alan: To be honest, I don't. I feel like you throw me into an assignment without any warning or any explanation of how the assignment fits into the larger picture. And I am afraid to come to you for help, since I know you don't like that. In the end I spend a lot of time feeling frustrated because I don't know where to start.

Frances: I think a lot of that has to do with my own style and how I like to work. I generally prefer to figure things out on my own. That style works well for me. But I am learning that not everyone has the same style. And so I need to get used to adapting to other ways of doing things, and to giving more instruction to people, when appropriate. I think I have a blind spot here.

Alan: I appreciate your willingness to take in this feedback

Frances: At the same time, I want you to understand that I can't always take you through every detail of an assignment. I need and expect that you will take some initiative and, over time, need less and less guidance from me.

Alan: I would like to get to the point where I can work more autonomously.

Frances: So why don't we agree that I will try to give you more guidance, and if I am not giving you enough, or too much, you will let me know. In addition, let's plan to check in on this topic in another few weeks to see how it's going.

Remember, looking from the outside in doesn't mean accepting all the blame. You can see in the sample dialogue that although Frances took responsibility for her own role in their difficult dynamic, she was still able to ask Alan to take responsibility for *his* behavior. Indeed, you can often set a good example by owning your own contribution to the problem, leading the other side to reflect and own his blind spots, too. But even if that doesn't happen, don't shy away from making yourself vulnerable. The payoff, in terms of your own growth and self-knowledge, is enormous. And you can do that *without* giving up on what it is that you want to say, while still holding on to your own perspective on the situation.

WALKING DOWN THE ROAD

In my work with clients, I find that helping them look from the outside in is both the most challenging and most rewarding way to grow. The payoff is proportional to the pain. I have deep respect and compassion for people who are willing to go down this road. If you are having trouble making this mental shift, try the following exercise: Imagine that all the feedback you are getting about yourself is true. Suspend disbelief momentarily and take what other people say at face value. And then ask yourself: *If* what I am being told were true, what would be the worst part of that? What would be scary about that? What would I need to do about that state of affairs?

It's nothing more than a thought experiment, spending five minutes to look at yourself from the outside in, even though you believe the feedback is untrue. Sometimes just taking those five minutes is enough to give you a powerful insight.

SUMMARY

Looking at yourself from the outside in can be a disorienting and even painful experience. Resisting it is natural. However, as a practice, it not only helps you get unstuck, but provides an opportunity to learn about your own behavior and derive lessons that can be applied to other situations as well. You don't need to make a radical change or totally transform your personality to benefit; even a little more self-awareness, leading to small changes in behavior, can have a major effect. Looking from the outside in offers a profound opportunity to learn and grow, so embrace it. Working with a trusted partner can help you overcome your resistance, allowing you to truly flex your mind.

Situations get stuck because of many factors that interact with one another. There is the other person's behavior, which is driven by the individual's own story, as discussed in Chapter Four. There is your own behavior, to which you are probably a bit blind. It was the intent of this chapter to help you see your own blind spots more clearly. But a third important variable is the overall context, the system within which both you and the other side are operating. Becoming aware of the system and its impact on your situation is the topic of Chapter Six.

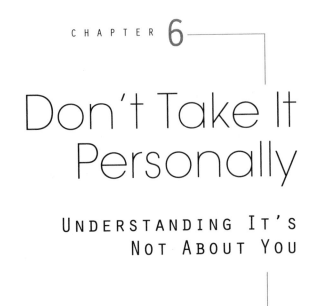

Don't Take It Personally

UNDERSTANDING IT'S NOT ABOUT YOU

Hans, the director of a technology team for a large investment bank, was fighting with Linda, a banker who was also his internal client. "She is constantly pushing me on deadlines," he said. "If I tell her a project will take two months, Linda says she needs it in one month. If I tell her it will take a month, she says she needs it in two weeks. Keeping Linda happy is a big part of my job, but no matter what I say or do, she is never satisfied."

Linda, for her part, was equally frustrated. "I never know how long a project really takes, and my external clients want answers *fast*. Hans gives me a date by which he can get the job done, but whenever I push him to see if he can speed things up, he is somehow able to get it done sooner. His initial timeline is not his real timeline. So I have no choice but to push him, because I need to get him to work toward his real deadline, not the one he gives me at first."

The conflict between Hans and Linda is indisputable, and each is experiencing sincere frustration with the other person. But as we will see in this chapter, the real driver of this conflict is not these two individuals. It's the roles they play inside their organization. In the business world, rarely are people working completely independently. Most of the time individuals are part of a larger team or organization and they are playing a role within that organization. Sometimes, when conflict arises, the tension exists independently of the personalities involved. It is the system and their roles within it that force Hans and Linda into conflict, not their particular tendencies.[1] Learning to recognize how the system creates conflict, and acquiring skills to address those conflicts, is a key part of flexing your mind and shifting perspective.

SYSTEMIC CONFLICT IS ROLE-BASED

It's hard to observe the system when you are inside it. We experience other people's behavior in a personal way. We discount or don't notice the role they are playing and instead attribute their behavior to "who they are."

Several years ago I was called for jury duty in Manhattan. I duly arrived at 9:00 a.m., desperately hoping that I would not be called to serve on a case, which would allow me to go home in a day or two. I entered an enormous room where hundreds of people were waiting. I had many questions about the process: the odds that I would be seated as a juror, the number of days I would spend in the potential juror pool before being released, what time we broke for lunch, etc.

The clerk behind a desk near the entrance seemed like the natural person to ask. I approached the desk and started talking to her, but she refused to answer my questions or engage with me in any way. She barely even looked at me. She simply gave me a form and said, "I will make an announcement in a few minutes." I felt frustrated and angry. Here I was, ripped out of my daily life against my will for three days or more by a legal system that my tax dollars pay for, and this clerk wouldn't even answer my questions! Not having much choice, I sat down and waited for the announcement.

The clerk's announcement was made at 9:15 a.m., by which time most of those called for jury duty had arrived. During the intervening fifteen minutes, however, literally dozens of potential jurors had approached the desk with questions, mostly the same ones I had tried to ask. And in each case the clerk replied in the same way: "I will make an announcement in a few minutes."

When I finally heard the announcement, which was long and extremely thorough, I realized why the clerk had refused to answer. All the information I needed was provided, and every single question was anticipated and answered. I no longer felt frustrated or upset about how the clerk behaved.

I subsequently reflected on my initial feelings of anger and the shift that took place not long after. I realized that initially I had taken the clerk's behavior personally and interpreted it as rudeness. In truth, there was nothing at all personal in how she was treating me. Rather, my interaction with the clerk was a product of the system. It was far more efficient to tell everyone the same thing at once, rather than having dozens or hundreds of conversations individually. Thus, the system was created to channel people's questions into the group announcement. This allowed one person to handle the huge volume of questions, rather than having several staff members behind the desk repeating the same information over and over. The system created temporary frustration for me but was more efficient overall. Once I saw the *systemic* nature of the interaction, it not only didn't upset me; it actually made sense.

Systemic tensions come in many shapes and sizes. Let's review a few of the most common systemically driven conflicts.

COMPETING INCENTIVES

One common driver of systemic tension is the competing set of incentives motivating employees working in an organization. To appreciate how the system pits Hans and Linda against each other, we need to step back and examine the individual role each of them is playing within the wider context.

Linda is part of a team that manages relationships with external clients of the bank. These clients generate millions of dollars of revenue for the bank, making these relationships extremely important. They can easily take their business to a competitor bank if they are unhappy, and many threaten to do so when they are not satisfied with the service they are getting. (And everyone knows that other banks are waiting in the wings to steal a client when they see an opportunity.)

Clients use this leverage to make extreme demands, putting tremendous pressure on Linda. Losing a client would be bad for the bank in general and disastrous for Linda personally. Thus, she is exceptionally motivated to do anything and everything she can to keep her clients satisfied, which includes leaning very hard on her internal technology team to meet a client's demands, even when those demands are extreme.

Hans, in turn, heads a technology team that serves a number of different groups within the bank. His "clients" are not actually external clients, but internal business units such as Linda's, which use technology to serve their external clients. Hans has several different Lindas that assign him work, and he is responsible to each one of them for the projects to which he committed, within the time frame he promised. Naturally, each internal client feels her project is the most important and pushes for the fastest turnaround. With a limited number of people on his team, Hans is forced to prioritize the various requests and try to balance each internal client's needs.

Moreover, internal clients, including Linda, sometimes misunderstand or misjudge what an external client's request requires. The external client may ask for something that sounds simple but will actually take Hans and his team many hours or even days to deliver. Therefore, Hans must be careful about committing to deadlines, and he must frequently resist pressure from his internal clients for a faster turnaround when doing so would jeopardize other projects that already have resources committed to them and a delivery date.

Given this context, it is easy to see how Hans and Linda are caught in a systemic tension. Hans is trying to avoid being penalized for missing a deadline. The only thing worse than saying no to a client is saying yes but then failing to deliver as promised. As someone who works in IT, Hans knows that it's difficult to predict exactly how long something will take. There are always unexpected bumps in the road, and time must be allocated to deal with these circumstances. Although project specifications may be clear and precise, sometimes the internal client changes her mind after seeing the implementation of her initial request. Other times new circumstances or information lead the external clients to alter their request after work has begun.

Both of these possibilities create a reasonable likelihood of project specifications changing midstream, adding to the time it takes to complete a project. Because Hans is responsible for making sure things get done correctly and on time, he builds in a cushion when giving a deadline, with the expectation that things will either get changed or go wrong and need to be fixed along the way. This is not a manifestation of Hans's personality; other technologists would have no choice but to operate in the same manner.

Linda's job, on the other hand, is to maintain a hyper-focus on her clients. She doesn't know about the other tasks Hans must juggle, and it's not her job to worry about them. Her job is to serve her clients, period. She is under tremendous pressure to deliver what they want quickly, and she fears that if she is not fast enough she might lose business to a competitor. And the pressure is not just from the client. Linda's manager is demanding that she get clients what they want when they want it. Moreover, as a person without expertise in technology, Linda is not in a position to objectively judge how long the work should take. All she knows is that she has to find a way to say yes to the client.

In response to this demanding context, Linda puts pressure on Hans and asks for deadlines that might be unrealistic. It's not because Linda is pushy as an individual; it's because her job requires her to advocate for her client's needs. That is what her clients, her manager, and the bank overall expect her to do.

The systemic tension between Linda and Hans then builds on itself. Because Hans knows there likely will be new demands added once the project is under way, he builds in an even larger time cushion. This decision allows him room to maneuver and the ability to concede later by forgoing the cushion and agreeing to a shorter timeline.

Yet over time, Hans's scheduling method has changed Linda's behavior. Because Linda knows there is a cushion built in and has seen Hans sometimes accept an accelerated timeline when pressed, she exerts even more pressure in order to force Hans to abandon the cushion and agree to get things done sooner. Indeed, she may also build in a "reverse cushion" herself by initially demanding a more aggressive timeline than she truly needs so that she can make a concession to Hans and ultimately get the deadline she really wants.

When this cyclical dynamic is played out repeatedly, it leads to an "arms race" of sorts, with the cushions getting bigger and the demands becoming more aggressive, such that any discussions about deadlines can become quite emotional and feel very personal. But it's important to notice that the conflict between Hans and Linda is not personal. If we were to replace Hans with a different programmer and Linda with a different banker, this conflict of roles would still exist. The system puts different corporate roles into conflict, regardless of the personalities occupying those roles.

THE BENEFITS OF COMPETING INCENTIVES

Far from being an accident or a coincidence, corporations often deliberately establish competing incentives, ensuring systemic tensions within the company. Why? The intention is for the competing incentives to motivate people or departments to work harder to achieve their goal to the utmost, with the corporation as a whole reaping the benefits.

Consider, for example, a private wealth management division within a bank. Private wealth managers receive money from wealthy individuals and invest it on their behalf. Their goal is to optimize these investments for the benefit of the client, including tax implications, inheritance issues, and tolerance of risk. These divisions produce significant revenue for banks, so keeping these clients happy (while adding new ones) is of the utmost importance.

At the same time, regulators realize the importance of monitoring the flow of capital inside the banking system in order to fight against money laundering, terrorism, and drug trafficking. Banks now operate under strict rules, with stiff penalties for violations. Some of these rules impact how the bank must treat its clients. Certain patterns of transactions in an account trigger a need to investigate the possibility of illegal activity. As frustrating and stressful as that may be for the client, failing to investigate puts the bank at risk for a compliance violation, even if there was no illegal activity.

How does the bank make sure both of these important goals

are achieved? A private wealth division will typically separate its compliance department from its sales department and provide different incentives for each. The incentive for the sales department is to grow sales as much as possible, in order to maximize income. The incentive for the compliance department is to aggressively monitor and investigate any suspicious activity by clients, thereby minimizing risk to the bank. Each department has a single-minded focus, which in turn allows the bank to balance the need to serve clients with the need to adhere strictly to regulations.

The test for this approach, which sounds fairly straightforward, is how it handles the ambiguous cases where it's not immediately clear what the regulations require. For example, there may be a gray area of activity that is not overtly suspicious, so it is not clear that an intrusive investigation is warranted. There is cost and risk associated with investigating (both in time and resources), but also the potential to damage a client relationship through the mere suggestion that the client is doing something illegal. At the same time, there is cost and risk associated with *not* investigating, because if the activity ultimately is discovered by a regulator and declared problematic, the bank may face penalties and fines for failing to report it, with the bank then suffering reputational damage as well.

So, how should gray situations get handled? Again, the bank wants to address both sides of this equation and find the optimal balance between protecting client relationships and maximizing sales, on the one hand, and minimizing reputational and regulatory risk, on the other. The competing incentives are designed to drive both compliance and sales to aggressively seek solutions that meet their respective needs—protecting the bank while simultaneously protecting customer relationships. Each department can vigorously advocate for its side of the equation and, by collaborating with each other, find creative solutions that would otherwise be overlooked.

At least, that is the hope. In reality, things don't always go smoothly, and it's easy to see why. Steve, a private wealth salesperson, has been taught to focus on sales. Selling can't happen without a relationship, and so Steve has an enormous incentive to both build and protect his client relationships. These relationships usually take years to establish, and the last thing Steve wants to do is upset a client by investigating an activity that falls into a "gray area." In addition, Steve personally benefits from the upside of making a sale by receiving a commission; the potential downside risk of investigation is shared by the bank overall. The upside benefit is immediate; the downside consequences may not emerge until years later.

Contrast that with the incentives facing Corinne, a compliance officer. Her mandate is to protect the bank from facilitating client activity that is legally problematic. The risk of a regulatory sanction is real, and even cases without clear-cut wrongdoing must be investigated thoroughly. The potential harm to the bank if something is not investigated and yet is ultimately found to be illegal is enormous. Corinne does not stand to benefit in any concrete way if the client is left alone. However, she might suffer huge personal career costs if she fails to investigate. The incentive for her, then, is not to take any chances and to investigate any and every case, however remote the risk of potentially illegal activity, in order to maximize her upside and minimize her downside. Imagine the following conversation:

Steve: I don't think an investigation is warranted here.

Corinne: We can't afford to take a chance. Your client is making a lot of cash withdrawals and wires to accounts overseas. The pattern is suspicious enough that we need to investigate.

Steve: He hasn't done anything wrong. Every transfer has been documented. It's not as if he is trying to evade paying his taxes. Besides, he is one of our best clients. I'm not about to jeopardize this relationship just because you have a bad feeling about someone.

Corinne: Maybe all you care about is your commission, but I'm here to protect the bank. If we don't investigate, we are jeopardizing our reputation and credibility with the regulatory agency, and I'm not prepared to do that. I think you are biased and your judgment is clouded.

Steve: You don't give a damn about relationships because you don't manage any!

Corinne: And you don't care about compliance because it's not your job on the line!

The issue here is the incentives each person faces. Personal attacks may be launched, as in this example, but it's not a personal matter. Replace Steve with a different salesperson and Corinne with a different compliance officer, and you are likely to get a similar debate.

It may be tempting to view this situation as a question of ethics and to say the compliance officer's overzealousness is ethically superior to the salesperson's reluctance to investigate. However, I believe that would be a mistake. While letting shady behavior go unchecked is obviously unethical, harassing law-abiding clients by investigating perfectly legal transactions just to protect the bank is not particularly virtuous or ethical. It is not a viable long-term strategy, either. The zealous investigation of clients who have done nothing wrong risks those clients taking their business to another bank that is more user-friendly.

Some people may argue that I have painted an extreme picture of the bank and the respective departments. Wouldn't salespeople such as Steve appreciate the risk to the bank (and to them personally) of suspicious activity going uninvestigated? Don't compliance officers such as Corinne understand that there is cost and risk associated with antagonizing clients? Yes and no. Indeed, many experienced salespeople and wise compliance officers will be able to see the big picture, ameliorating this tension. But it's hard to see the big picture when your own "small picture" is threatened. Neither Steve nor Corinne wants to take any chances when the stakes are high, and each will fight hard to protect his or her turf. Particularly where the situation is ambiguous and the rules are not completely clear, there is bound to be disagreement over what should be done and how these competing incentives should be balanced. And in those situations, conflict is likely to ensue.

The benefit of competing incentives depends on robust and constructive discussion occurring between people such as Steve and Corinne. That is the only way the bank can optimally balance its competing concerns. Such a discussion, as tense as it is likely to be, requires highly developed communication and conflict resolution skills, which makes learning to see the system vitally important. Otherwise, the conflict created by the system can destroy the very efficiencies it was designed to create. Later in this chapter I will show you how to navigate systemic conflicts with skill and confidence.

HIERARCHY

Hierarchy is another common driver of systemic tension in an organization. Here, the tension is not caused by differing incentives, but by the unequal power that the parties possess. The power imbalance has a dramatic impact on how the parties communicate (or fail to communicate).

Amelia is a senior partner at a prominent architectural design firm, having worked there for many years. Amelia works closely with Curt, an associate at the firm who will be reviewed for partnership at the end of the year. For Curt to "make partner," something he wants badly, he needs to receive a unanimous affirmative vote from all of the existing partners. Thus, it is essential for him to have a good reputation and relationship with each of the eight partners.

But tension has arisen between Amelia and Curt. Amelia is frustrated because Curt has fallen behind on some of his assignments. Curt is frustrated as well, because Amelia keeps asking him to do more work when he already has as many projects as he can handle. Here's my conversation with Amelia:

Me: What is your issue with Curt?

Amelia: Curt is not getting his work done on time. I ask him to do something for me, and he says he will, but then it turns out he has other commitments that prevent him from doing my work on time.

Me: Why do you think this is happening?

Amelia: I think Curt is just not good at managing his time.

Me: Have you raised the issue with him?

Amelia: I tried to. I told him, "If you are too busy to accept an assignment from me, tell me." But he doesn't. Instead he overcommits, and then things don't get done.

Contrast that with the following conversation with Curt:

Me: What is the issue with Amelia?

Curt: Amelia is one of the senior partners, and saying no to her is not a good strategy if you want to make partner. And the problem is not just Amelia—it's all of the partners. Because I have a lot of experience and they know me, everyone wants me to work on their engagements. And, whether they realize it or not, saying no to a partner when you are about to get voted on is risky. Any one of them can blackball me and block my partnership. So I basically have to say yes to everyone, and do the best that I can to juggle everything.

Me: Have you told this to Amelia?

Curt: Well, I tried to, but she said, "Don't worry about that. If you are too busy to take on something, I will understand." But I don't believe her. I heard that she voted against another associate nominated for partnership because she didn't feel he was "committed to the firm," whatever that means. The partnership meetings are confidential, so she—or any partner, for that matter—can stab me in the back and I would never know. Saying no to a partner is just too risky.

As you can see, the systemic tension here is caused by hierarchy. The system, which gives each partner tremendous power over the associates, creates an environment in which it is difficult for an associate to have an honest conversation with any of the partners. The power to deny a promotion creates fear on the part of the associates and inhibits communication.

Moreover, the partners may be oblivious to this imbalance. The mechanics of the system are such that the power is diffuse. Decisions are made by a vote; no single partner has the authority to promote an associate. Thus, all the partners legitimately believe that they are not so powerful that an associate should be afraid to be honest with them. But in reality, associates fear saying no.

Note that no individual is acting "badly" in this scenario. Amelia is not trying to intimidate Curt; her position as partner is itself intimidating. And Curt is not an indirect or evasive person by nature; his position of vulnerability as a candidate for partnership forces him to act that way to protect himself. Their roles are what cause the conflict, and this dynamic undoubtedly plays out with many different partners and many different associates. Changing the interpersonal dynamic isn't the key to unlocking this type of stuck situation; rather, it is changing, or at least discussing, the systemic dynamic at play.

Hierarchy is an extremely common cause of systemic tension. In a university department, tenured faculty members have much more power than junior, untenured faculty members on whom they will ultimately vote for tenure. The resulting power imbalance can lead to tension. In most corporations, an employee's promotions and future success depend on the approval of her boss, which also creates a power imbalance.

Hierarchy and power imbalances are not inherently bad. It makes sense for people with more experience and greater responsibilities to have more authority, and ultimately more power, than those with less experience and fewer responsibilities. Amelia, as a partner/owner of the firm, *should* have the ability to vote on future partners with whom she will need to work closely. The system is not necessarily flawed, but it will impact how people within the system interact and communicate. And learning how to manage those interactions is the skill we are discussing.

WORKING FOR A SUPERHERO

A third driver of systemic tension is something I refer to as the "superhero organization." These organizations are built around and reliant on a single individual. In such a context, there is an inevitable systemic effect on how people interact with this "superhero." One classic example occurs in many hedge funds.

Hedge funds are investment firms. They receive money from investors and are charged with investing that money to generate positive returns in excess of the broader market. It is a highly competitive business, and beating the market is difficult. Hedge funds that can generate consistent positive returns succeed and make huge sums of money for their employees; those that don't go out of business.

Many hedge funds are founded by a single person. This individual is the driver behind the firm: This person's name, reputation, and relationships are on the line, and it is this individual's personal skill in investing money that determines whether the fund will succeed or fail.

From a systemic point of view, a superhero organization has

a number of challenges. There are hierarchical tensions because there is an enormous power imbalance between the founder and everyone else. However, in this context that imbalance is even more acute. All of the employees are entirely dependent on the founder, on whose shoulders their livelihoods rest. And unlike Amelia and Curt's situation, the power to hire and fire is concentrated in a single individual.

The superhero, moreover, does not have a boss over him who might soften or equalize the power imbalance. That individual is above everyone else. If a typical hierarchy can be represented by vertical lines moving up the chain of command, a superhero organization is more like a wheel, with the superhero in the raised center of the circle and spokes radiating outward to the rest of the employees of the organization. And hedge funds can be quite small; a firm that manages billions of investor dollars may have fewer than twenty employees.

This creates a situation in which displeasing the boss can be a matter of professional life or death. Employees are often reluctant to say no or contradict the founder for fear of repercussions. Indeed, to a certain degree, currying favor with the superhero becomes part of everyone's job. Employees will often jockey to move their own position closer to the center of the wheel, since proximity to the superhero is a measure of status and allows that employee to influence the boss from up close.

Hedge funds are not the only superhero organizations. A surgical team headed by a star surgeon can function in the same way. Actors or other performers, as well as business celebrities such as Oprah Winfrey, Martha Stewart, or Donald Trump, who are a brand unto themselves, can be the superhero centers of their organizations. In all of these cases, the organization becomes focused on the individual, which creates systemic challenges.

PERSONALITIES WITHIN THE SYSTEM

It is possible to have both a personal issue and a systemic issue simultaneously making a situation challenging. In the jury duty example, on top of the systemic issue, the jury duty clerk might also have an abrasive personality, making the situation even more difficult to handle.

Consider the example of Amelia and Curt at the architectural design firm. Imagine that, in addition to Amelia being a partner who will get to vote on Curt's partnership, she also tends to be a self-centered and vindictive person. She doesn't like it when people say no to her, and she pushes hard when encountering resistance. And when Amelia doesn't get her way, she tends to exact retribution from the other person. Amelia might also be in denial about these personality traits—she is unable to look from the outside in, as described in Chapter Five. For Curt, this set of circumstances would constitute a perfect storm of conflict, in which the systemic power imbalance and Amelia's vindictive personality reinforce each other. That doesn't mean Curt can't find a way to successfully resolve conflict with Amelia, but it does mean that his challenge will be even greater, requiring Curt to have even more self-awareness and even stronger communication skills.

Mutually reinforcing personal and systemic challenges, leading to acute conflicts, are particularly common in superhero organizations. Indeed, these types of organizations will often begin to embody the personal flaws and foibles of the founder as organizational norms.

For example, imagine a clothing design firm that's built around a single superstar designer who happens to be averse to conflict. She avoids direct confrontation, even when doing so ends up harming the firm. This is a personal shortcoming for the founder and an area for interpersonal growth that would require her to look from the outside in.

But because the founder works in a superhero organization, it is difficult for her to get the feedback she would need to grow and learn to be better able to tolerate conflict. That is the systemic challenge—no one will confront her.

The reciprocal reinforcement of these personal and systemic issues occurs when the firm begins to replicate the personality of the conflict-averse founder. People will model their behavior after the boss, making them less likely to engage conflicts. When the firm is recruiting and hiring, there will be a bias toward candidates that fit within those norms, and for newly hired employees, those tendencies and norms will be reinforced by everyone already working there. And there is a huge disincentive for anyone to deviate from the founder's style and preferences—after all, she carries the firm on her shoulders and can fire anyone at will. Even outside customers would be happy to go along with a founder's peculiarities, provided she is providing them with designs that are successful. Thus the systemic challenge and the personality challenge each make the other issue more acute.

The superhero context has particular relevance for the skill of looking from the outside in. As discussed in Chapter Five, we all struggle to see ourselves as others see us, and superheroes are no exception. I have coached many of them, and they are typically in denial about their personal flaws. This is not surprising—it's especially difficult for them to see from the outside in since the people closest to them are disinclined to offer candid and critical feedback. In fact, the successful ones receive tremendous positive reinforcement telling them they are doing great.

Superhero founders often don't consider how the system of the type of firm they manage creates a barrier to their own personal self-awareness. They hold so much power that they run the risk of no one sharing a contrary opinion. No one will want to tell the emperor that he has no clothes, so to speak. Indeed, no one will even want to describe the system as inhibiting honesty. Thus, the personal and the systemic issues reinforce each other and make the scenario even more resistant to constructive change.

WHO CARES?

We've seen that in many difficult situations, it is the roles people are playing that cause the conflict. We've also seen that systemic tensions are common in the professional world and can be caused by factors such as competing incentives, hierarchy, and superhero organizations.

But how does knowing all this help you in your stuck situations? Why bother paying attention to the systemic aspect of the conflict? Here's why.

First of all, seeing the system allows you to *depersonalize the situation*. Everything in this book shows you how flexing your mind and shifting your thinking will shift your capacity for engaging constructively with the other side. Detaching and depersonalizing the conflict helps you to cool off emotionally, so you can think more clearly. When I feel that the jury duty clerk is personally slighting me, it is difficult for me to operate at my best. If Hans believes Linda is personally disrespecting him, he won't be able to negotiate with her in an optimal way. However, once you are able to understand the system, you can sidestep the emotional trigger and recognize, "Okay, this is not directed at me personally and I don't have to take it personally." Depersonalizing doesn't mean stopping to care or giving up. It simply means you can step back and see the forest, not just the tree that is causing your grief.

Second, seeing the system also allows you to *see the other side differently*. A systemic mindset allows one to view the other side as people struggling inside a context that is pressuring them. This, in turn, fosters empathy. Rather than demonizing the other side, we humanize them and are able to understand why they are acting that way. Humanizing the other and empathizing with their plight can be quite liberating. It unlocks our skills of communication and collaboration.

Third, seeing the system allows one to *consider alternative courses of action* within the system. Not every stuck situation can or should be addressed one-on-one. For example, imagine you are Corinne, the bank compliance officer. And suppose that you feel certain client activity requires investigation, yet the salesperson working with that client is vigorously resisting any investigation for fear of antagonizing the client. If you are able to understand the systemic aspects, not only can you depersonalize the situation and feel empathy for the salesperson, but you might consider escalating the issue to someone more senior in the sales department. A senior manager is probably better able to see both sides of the issue and give a more balanced perspective on the right course of action.

Finally, seeing the system allows you to *make the system itself a discussable topic.* In the previous example, Hans might actually discuss the competing pressures he and Linda are under as a way to address their conflict. Once you see it, you can directly address it.

WHY IT'S HARD

Recognizing the systemic dimension to your own conflict, while fairly simple to explain in the abstract, can be quite difficult to achieve in practice. I believe there are two layers to this challenge, one cognitive and one emotional.

There is a cognitive tendency toward attributing other people's behavior to their personality, not their role or circumstances, that psychologists call the *fundamental attribution error.*[2]

Imagine you see someone at the airport yelling at a gate attendant. You don't know anything else about the situation; you simply can observe that this person is yelling. What are you likely to conclude? If you are like most people, your tendency will be to say that the person doing the yelling is aggressive. You are much less likely to say that the person was just treated badly and is responding to the situation. The fundamental attribution error refers to the tendency to overly attribute people's behavior to an aspect of their personality, rather than the context they are confronted with.

Interestingly, people tend toward the reverse assumption regarding their own behavior. If you found yourself yelling at someone in the airport, you are much more likely to explain your behavior as a response to what's being done to you, rather than as evidence that you are an aggressive person.

Delving into why this bias exists is beyond the scope of this book. For our purposes it is sufficient to recognize that it is an entrenched tendency. When Hans is pressured by Linda to give her a faster deadline, he is much more likely to say "Linda is aggressive" than to say "Linda is under tremendous pressure." When Amelia sees Curt overcommitting and falling behind in his work, she is much more likely to say that "Curt doesn't manage his time well" than she is to say "As an associate, Curt feels pressured to say yes to every partner." Because this is how we naturally respond to and interpret the situations we find ourselves in, we are biased against seeing the system. In addition to this cognitive bias against seeing how the larger context contributes to getting us stuck, I believe there is an emotional dimension inhibiting people from seeing the system. Recalling my firsthand experience with jury duty, I was extremely angry at how the clerk was ignoring me. And, at least initially, I was too upset to think it through clearly. Of all people, I ought to have been able to understand why the clerk behaved the way she did. Intellectually, I should have been able to recognize the system in action and use that insight to unlock my own skills. I did eventually get there on my own, but only after spending some time cooling off, after which my brain was again working at full capacity. And I wonder if someone had come up to me just at that moment and said, "Well, don't take it personally, it's just the system," how I might have reacted. I probably would have said, "The system is not an excuse for this person's behavior. She is abusing the power she has over me to force me to be here. It's totally unfair, and this person is simply rude!"

It isn't just me that reacts this way, because I see it happen with my clients as well. As a coach, I am an outsider to my client's organization, and it's relatively easy for me to see the system. Yet when I confront my client with the systemic dimension, I sometimes encounter fierce resistance. Consider the following conversation with Hans, from the example that began this chapter, in which I try to show him the role Linda is playing within the system of their large investment bank:

Me: Hans, why do you think Linda is pushing you so hard on the deadline?

Hans: Because she doesn't care about anyone else's priorities, only her own.

Me: What are her priorities?

Hans: She wants to make sure her clients are first in line and get things right away. But I have to balance that with all of the other clients I am serving.

Me: So her clients are her priority. Isn't that her job—to make her clients her priority?

Hans: Yes, but she should still be reasonable about it. She is being totally self-centered.

Me: Why isn't she giving you reasonable deadlines?

Hans: I think that's just her style. A lot of people around here are like that—they are arrogant and think that they are the most important person in the world, and they push aggressively to get what they want.

Me: Think about this: Who is putting pressure on Linda?

Hans: What difference does that make?

Me: Well, understanding the challenges she faces might help you negotiate with her.

Hans: I supposed her external clients are, and probably her boss.

Me: So, in a sense, she is responding to pressure on her by putting pressure on you?

Hans: Yes, you could say that. But does that justify her behavior?

Let's pause this dialogue. As you can see, I have tried to get Hans to recognize, on a cognitive level, that there is a systemic aspect to the conflict. But Hans continues to resist throughout. Why? Because seeing the system feels frustrating. If Hans sees the system then, maybe, he doesn't get to be as angry as he feels. After all, if Linda is just trying to do her best in a harsh, high-pressure system, doesn't that mean that Hans has to simply accept it?

Here's my answer: No, it doesn't. All of us, including Hans, can still have our feelings. If Linda is treating him badly, he can be angry. If Curt is feeling pressured or bullied by the partners at his architectural design firm, he can still be upset, despite recognizing that they may be unaware of the power imbalance the system has created. One's feelings don't have to evaporate just because the situation is systemic. However, Hans *might* feel less angry if he could see the system. Curt might feel less frustrated if he saw the system. I certainly know that I felt less frustrated once I was able to identify how the system caused the jury clerk to act the way she did.

In my dialogue with Hans, he asked another important question: Are you justifying her behavior? Are you saying Linda is off the hook? Why is what she is doing okay?

This is a recurring theme in this book. And as before, my answer here is the same. Recognizing the systemic conflict does not transform bad behavior into good behavior. In any of the examples cited in this chapter, the various people are still responsible for their actions, good, bad, or otherwise. Linda does not get a free pass. There is an important distinction between *understanding* the systemic impact on other people and its role in driving their behavior, as opposed to *justifying* their behavior. You might accept the other person's behavior once you see the system, as I did in my jury duty experience. But you might not. And that's fine.

Recognizing the system does not justify anyone's behavior. It doesn't make it okay for Linda to mislead Hans about her true deadline to get more out of him, for example. The point here is not to justify; it is to understand. Once you understand the other person's behavior, you are in a much better position to respond to it.

IDENTIFYING YOUR SYSTEMIC CONFLICT

So how can you know if you are caught in a systemic conflict, especially when it feels so personal?

You've probably had the experience of looking out from high up and seeing everything for miles around. It may be from a mountaintop, an airplane, or the top floor of a skyscraper. Regardless, from way up high, you can see far and wide and get an overall view of the situation. Military commanders recognize that the view from above a battlefield is far more strategic than the view from below, which is why reconnaissance flights, satellite photographs, and unmanned drones with cameras are so important in a modern military. It allows a person to "zoom out" and see the whole picture, something that is hard to do from up close.

This metaphor captures what you need to do. The wide-angled "view from above" is the system within which you and your counterpart are operating. It's important to cultivate the ability to zoom out, and to do so, you need to build your capacity to see the system and the roles within it that you and others are playing. Identifying the systemic dimension to your conflict is a powerful mental shift.

There are clues that may indicate a systemic issue has arisen. One is to ask yourself: *Is this a familiar dynamic?* Looking at other people who have had a similar issue can reveal how the system creates conflict. Consider whether this conflict has played out before, with different players. If so, there may be a systemic issue. Corinne might ask herself if she has fought with other salespeople, or if any of her compliance colleagues have had similar problems with members of the sales force.

Systemic issues may become more evident if you try to *define people in terms of the role they play,* rather than who they are as individuals. If Amelia were to say, "I have a problem with an associate who is about to be voted on for partnership" instead of "I have a problem with Curt," she might notice the systemic dimension. Similarly, if Hans were to say, "There is an issue between a business person and an IT person," instead of "Linda and I don't get along," he might more readily see how their roles put them in conflict. In your own stuck situation, ask yourself, "What role do I play in the system? What role does the other side play?"

Because other parties may be putting pressure on you or the other side, the system becomes more apparent once you *bring other players into your "mental map"* of the situation. If Hans were to consider the impact of Linda's clients on her, he could begin to see how the system was heavily influencing her responses to him. If Amelia expands her thinking to consider how Curt might be interacting with other partners in the firm, she could start to see how her status as a partner creates a power imbalance and how that situation, not Curt's inability to manage his time, is the cause of his overcommitments.

A useful way to expand your mental map is to create an actual map of the conflict. Here is a simple exercise: Take a blank piece of paper and fold it in half. In the center of the page, just to the left of the fold, write your own name. Also in the center of the page, but just to the right of the fold, write the name of the person with whom you are having your conflict. Then draw a line from you to the other person.

What you have drawn so far is a map of the conflict with just the two parties involved, with the line between you representing the relationship and interaction you have. Now it's time to add in other people. On your half of the map, add in all the different people who are having an effect on you in this situation, as well as people who are impacted by you in this situation. You can write their names above your name, if they are higher up in the hierarchy than you, or lower down on the paper, if they are lower in the hierarchy, or off to the side if the relationship is of a peer nature. Draw a line connecting you to each of these people, and similarly draw a line between any two of these people if they interact with each other. Having mapped out your situation, now do the same on the other side. Add in the names of any parties you can think of that impact your counterpart, and connect with lines anyone who interacts with each other.

Having drawn your map of the system, ask yourself, "Who is exerting influence on whom in this situation? What pressures might my counterpart be under that are causing him to act this way?" You may be surprised at how clear the systemic nature of your conflict now becomes.

Finally, to help identify the systemic conflict, *humanize the other person* and assume that the individual is responding in a reasonable way to certain challenges. While the other person's behavior may appear unreasonable, that is often because the system applies unreasonable pressures, and so reasonable people behave unreasonably.

Consider the following example. You are on your way to the

airport and get stuck in traffic. Your flight leaves at three, and by the time you get to the airport, it's already 2:32 p.m. Miraculously, there is no line at security, so if you are able to run quickly you should make your flight on time.

You approach the counter to check in for the flight, at which point the gate attendant tells you, "I'm sorry, but I can't check you in—it's less than thirty minutes before the flight." You protest that you've bought a ticket and there is no line at security, and that no one will be harmed if she lets you check in now. But it's all to no avail. The gate attendant repeats, "I'm sorry, but I am not allowed to check you in. It's a federal regulation that flights are closed thirty minutes before, and I just can't help you."

This is clearly an infuriating situation (and, sadly, a real-life example I experienced back in the days before I starting checking in and printing my boarding pass at home). Why should the flight be closed thirty minutes before? Why doesn't the system give the gate attendant discretion to make an exception? Why aren't the customer's needs given more priority?

These are all valid questions that deserve answers. But here is the question I pose to you now: Did the gate attendant, as an individual, behave unreasonably? Consider her situation. She did not create the rule, she was merely enforcing it. Even if she were able to do the check-in inside the thirty-minute window, there would likely be consequences for her if she did so. She might lose her job and could possibly face legal penalties for subverting a security regulation.

Is it unreasonable behavior, then, on the gate attendant's part, to refuse to check you in? I don't think it is. Certainly the *system* may be unreasonable. Many security rules don't seem to have a purpose, something I am reminded of every time I fly. I don't know if closing the flight thirty minutes before departure truly makes us safer. But I don't think pushing back on the individual gate attendant is the answer. She was doing her job, and if most reasonable people would do the same, there is no point in attacking her. Once you recognize the role that the system plays, you can engage in a more constructive dialogue. While in this case, it's not clear that dialogue would change the outcome, it might help you achieve a better overall result—such as being rebooked on the next flight as seamlessly as possible.

HAVING THE CONVERSATION

When dealing with a systemically created conflict, it's important to do your homework. Before talking to the other side, you need to flex your mind and look for a similar dynamic with other people. Once you've humanized rather than demonized the other side, defined each side's roles, and mapped out the organizational pressure each side is facing, you are ready to have a conversation.

Here are a few pieces of advice to help you use your systemic awareness to make the conversation more constructive:

➤ *Acknowledge the other person's role and the difficulty the person is facing in that role.* This doesn't mean you are legitimating what they've done. It simply means you both understand and can empathize with the pressures they are under. You can invite people to clarify and describe further the stresses and challenge they face, both to make sure you understand their situation and to allow them an opportunity to "vent."

In the previous example of Corinne from the bank's compliance department and Steve from sales, Steve might say to Corinne, "I understand that you are responsible for protecting the bank and making sure all regulations are complied with. And if anything goes wrong, you as the compliance person will be the first person to be blamed." Steve might ask Corinne to share with him whatever frustrations she feels in playing this role.

▷ *Describe the role each of you plays in this conflict.* The other person may not notice the systemic aspect of the conflict at all. Therefore, you should make clear how it is not merely individuals but their roles that are in tension with one another inside a broader system.

Amelia might say to Curt, "I think that one of the challenges we both face is that as an aspiring partner who will be voted on this year, you probably find it hard to say no to me or any other partner for fear of displeasing us. From my side, I need to know that I can ask you for things and that you will give me timelines that you will fulfill. But the fact that there is a power imbalance here makes this tricky for both of us."

▷ *Make this situation work for everyone, not just your own side.* While you might think it is obvious, you need to explicitly state for the other side's benefit that you want their needs to be met together with your own. Making that your express goal is powerful and can help reduce defensiveness on the other side.

Here is a conversation between Hans and Linda, in which Hans tried to integrate all of the aforementioned advice:

Hans: Linda, I know you are under pressure from your client to get this project done right away.

Linda: You bet I am. You know how clients are—they want it yesterday.

Hans: Definitely. And I know that you feel the timeline I gave you before was exaggerated and included too much "cushion." Is that right?

Linda: Yes. You guys always pad your timelines, and in this case we can't afford that. I need to get back to the client with a quick turnaround date—that's what "customer focused" means.

Hans: I understand that you are trying to deliver for clients, and that in this case you needed something done quickly. I have pressures on my end as well. I have other internal clients that I need to serve, and commitments that I have already made that I need to keep. So we are both under the gun right now. Naturally, we are on the same team. We both want to deliver high-quality work, and we both want it done as fast as possible. I think one of the challenges is that we come at this situation from opposite sides. You are focused on your clients and your deadlines, which makes perfect sense. I am focused on making sure my team can deliver a high-quality product, which also makes sense. And because we are focusing on different parts of the overall picture, we get into conflict. In fact, I think this tension isn't about Hans and Linda, but about IT and business units more generally. What do you think?

Linda: Well, that makes sense. But I still need to deliver for my clients.

Hans: Of course. And that's my goal as well. Here's how I think we can frame the challenge: How do we find the right balance between meeting the client's expectations, on the one hand, and being realistic with the client, on the other? I know you are pressuring me because the client is pressuring you. I realize that it's not personal. I want you to understand that when I push back on you, it's not because I don't want to help—it's because it's my job to make sure things get done right and to be realistic with my clients about what we can do and by when.

Linda: Well, what about my client's expectations?

Hans: I think the goal should be for you and me to find a balance between accommodating the client and setting realistic expectations with them. Because if you are able to get me to say yes but it's not done on time or correctly, the client will still be unhappy. And if I get you to back off, but the client is angry and withdraws his business, I have also failed. We are on the same side here, although sometimes it feels as if we are pulling in opposite directions.

Linda: I see your point.

Once Hans and Linda both can see the systemic tension, they are in a much better frame of mind for problem solving. What should come next in this conversation is a robust discussion of possible solutions to this challenge. Beyond simply agreeing to a deadline, they might come up with a creative solution, such as delivering to the client a demo of the final product and soliciting feedback. This solution would take Hans much less time to produce while still allowing Linda to respond quickly to the client. But whatever the solution is, both the relationship and the communication between Hans and Linda will be much better once the systemic tension has been explicitly acknowledged.

SUMMARY

Organizations create structures and policies that allow them to more successfully achieve their goals. Establishing competing incentives between departments allows organizations to optimize the balance between conflicting goals. Creating hierarchy allows organizations to give greater power and responsibility to those with more skill and experience. Superhero organizational structures are designed to give a central individual (whether a surgeon, fund manager, designer, etc.) maximum autonomy and support, which in turn fosters the success of the entire organization.

At the same time, these organizational policies and structures inevitably create systemic tensions that impact the individuals working within them. These tensions can feel intensely personal, notwithstanding that they are driven by the organization and not the individuals. In order for the organization to function optimally, individuals need the ability to flex their minds and see the view from above, recognizing how the system is driving conflict. Shifting perspective in this way allows the system to be acknowledged and explicitly discussed, and it sets the stage for constructive dialogue and creative problem solving.

The next chapter explores shifting perspective from the opposite extreme. Is it possible to shift so far toward the other side's view that you lose your own view in the process? And if so, what can be done to correct that tendency? Addressing these important questions is our next task.

Don't Lose Yourself

MAINTAINING BALANCE

Edward and Helen were both sales representatives at an investment bank. Each received sales leads—names of prospective clients—from their manager, Maurice, and each was tasked with meeting with prospects and persuading them to invest with the firm. The sales reps were each compensated based on the number of new clients they closed, and, as such, the quality of the sales leads that each of them received was a major driver of their individual success.

Edward noticed that many of the best leads were being given to Helen. He raised the issue with Maurice, saying that he felt he was not getting his fair share of sales leads. Maurice listened to his concerns and promised that the next major lead would go to him and not to Helen.

The following week, however, when the name of a hugely wealthy potential client was given to Maurice, he again passed the lead on to Helen. Feeling frustrated, Edward again raised the issue with Maurice as follows:

Edward: Maurice, I want to talk about the prospect that you just passed on to Helen.

Maurice: Okay.

Edward: I thought we agreed that the next major lead would go to me. I can't close business if you don't give me leads.

Maurice: Hold on. This lead is a huge opportunity for our group. This client has enormous potential, and I didn't want to take any chances.

Edward: I can close big clients.

Maurice: Helen has more experience than you do. Isn't that true?

Edward: Yes, a little.

Maurice: But that makes a difference.

Edward: I suppose so.

Maurice: Besides, the most important thing is to make sure we land the client, not who gets the sales commission. I want to do what is best for the firm—don't you think that's fair?

Edward: Of course.

Maurice: This is a client that needs a certain touch. I think you can be a bit formal sometimes, and I think that Helen will do a better job than you closing the business.

Edward: Hmm. I guess there is some truth in that.

Maurice: If I were to pass on a name like this to you, and for whatever reason you don't close the business, it would look very bad for you. I am protecting you from the possibility of a major screwup. Don't worry; you'll get your chance when the time comes. For now, I am asking you to be a team player and defer to my judgment here.

Edward left the conversation unsure of what to do. He believed his career was stalling, and he did not know what steps to take in response. He felt stuck.

Edward reached out to me for help, and we had the following exchange:

Me: What is the problem?

Edward: I don't know. I feel that my manager, Maurice, is giving the best sales leads to Helen, the other salesperson on the team. And this matters a lot, because our compensation is based on how much business we close, and how much business we close is driven by how many leads we get. But I don't think there's anything I can do. I mean, Maurice's thinking makes a lot of sense.

Me: Have you spoken to Maurice about it?

Edward: Yes, I have. And after that he promised me that I would get the next big lead, but then when a big opportunity arose the following week, he again gave it to Helen.

Me: Did you ask him why?

Edward: I did. He explained that he had good reasons for his decision.

Me: Like what?

Edward: He said that he thought Helen would do a better job closing this client than I would. He mentioned that she has more experience, which is true. I've been doing this job for five years; she's been doing it for six. He also said that I am too formal sometimes, which is also true. And he wanted to do what was best for the firm, so I should be a team player and let him decide.

Me: Do you think he acted for the good of the firm?

Edward: Yeah, I guess so. Also, Maurice's compensation is based on how much business our team closes, irrespective of which salesperson does the closing. So his incentive is to just direct the lead to whomever he thinks will do the best job, regardless of whether he is dividing things equally between employees. And Maurice knows Helen better, because she has been on his team for four years, and I have been with him for only two years. He is more comfortable with her, and therefore he gives her the best leads.

Me: What do you think you should do?

Edward: Well, he is my manager, and I don't want to have a major screwup. And what he is saying has some merit. Maybe I should just wait it out until he thinks I am ready to tackle a big lead. I just wish he'd give me a chance.

Edward is in a stuck situation. Normally I would advise someone in a stuck situation to flex his mind and shift perspective. However, that's not the problem here. If anything, it's the opposite—Edward has flexed his mind, to an extreme. In our conversation, Edward demonstrated a deep understanding of the situation from other points of view. He is able to tell Maurice's story: Maurice wants to do what is best for the firm, he feels Helen's style works better with this client, and he's more comfortable with Helen. Edward is able to look at himself from the outside in and is open to feedback that his style might, at times, be too formal, and he is willing to work to improve in that area. He is even able to see the systemic aspect of the situation. Edward understands that although Maurice, as a manager, should try to assign leads evenly between employees, Maurice's personal compensation is highest if he assigns the best leads to Helen, who he thinks will do a better job. (Whether or not that's true, it's what Maurice believes.)

The problem is that rather than confronting Maurice's story, Edward is deferring to it, to his own detriment. Yes, Helen had more experience—but Edward had significant experience, too, having worked at the firm for five years. And Maurice had gone back on a promise. Edward swept his own story under the rug, instead focusing on Maurice's account.

Edward's case raises an interesting question: Is it possible that by shifting perspective, a person can virtually lose his ability to assert his own point of view? And if so, are there ways people can fight against this tendency and protect themselves?

THE PROBLEM

So far, most of this book has focused on overcoming our resistance to shifting perspective. This is indeed the most common problem: Most people only see things their own way. Thus, the challenge is to flex one's mind, to see *beyond* one's own perspective, and to take in other points of view.

However, there are people who have, at least in some cases, the opposite problem. When confronting a stuck situation, they tend to empathize too much with the other side and go too far in telling the other person's story. As a result, they have a diminished capacity to critically assess the other person's perspective, and they also undermine their ability to assert their own side of the story.

Some people are excessively empathetic because they lack confidence in their analytical ability in a particular area. This may lead them to feel easily swayed by someone else's story. Dylan was a massage therapist whose office lease was up for renewal. Given the downturn in the economy and the large number of vacancies in his building, he was not expecting his rent to go up at all. Indeed, if anything he thought his rent might be reduced, given the weak office rental market.

When he was sent a new lease with a standard 4 percent increase in his rent, he became quite frustrated. He knew other buildings had similar spaces available for less. He was insulted that the building would treat a long-term tenant this way, and he refused to sign the lease. After a number of e-mails back and forth, Dylan had a meeting with the building manager. The conversation went as follows:

Dylan: I don't understand why you raised my rent. The market is down, not up.

Manager: Look, this is standard policy.

Dylan: Why?

Manager: Consider the situation from our point of view. Our costs are constantly going up. Electricity, heating fuel, tax rates—all of these keep rising. We need to be able to cover our costs. Don't you think everyone deserves to make a decent living?

Dylan: Of course.

Manager: Also, we have tenants that stay in this building for a long time. In some years the market rises, some years it falls. We raise the rent by a standard amount, 4 percent, every year.

Dylan: I see your point. But I could find another office for cheaper.

Manager: Do you really want to go through the hassle of doing that? Besides, you would be surprised at the hidden expenses associated with moving—it will end up costing you more. And the other building is probably going to raise the rent on you next year anyway, so how much did you save in the end?

Dylan: I didn't think about that.

Manager: Of course you didn't; it's not your area of expertise. But I have been managing buildings for twenty years, so you can believe what I am saying is true. I have a lot of experience with things like this.

Dylan: Well, you certainly know more about this than I do. I guess what you are saying makes sense.

In this example, there are lots of counterarguments Dylan could have made. For example, other buildings are giving lower rents and free months to existing tenants; why can't this building match those offers? Or, while he as a tenant has costs associated with moving, the building will also have costs associated with finding a new tenant, including advertising the space and hiring a broker. Moreover, it could take many months to fill his unit, resulting in many months of lost revenue. The building has many incentives not to raise Dylan's rent, thereby avoiding the risk of losing him as a tenant altogether. Dylan should be listening to the manager's argument, considering it critically, and pushing back on it where appropriate. But Dylan does not do that; instead, he essentially buys into the manager's point of view.

Dylan is at risk of overempathizing with the other side's story and underasserting his own. Of course, he might not react this way in every situation; where Dylan feels he has expertise, he may be much more assertive in defending his own point of view. But here at least, in his conversation with building management, Dylan abandons his own logic and adopts the logic of his counterpart.

Dylan's lack of confidence impairs his ability to think critically and evaluate his counterpart's perspective. Other types of people struggle to hold on to their stories for different reasons. Some individuals feel emotional pressure to accept the other side's story, even as they are aware of the cognitive flaws in that position.

Lynn was an IT manager for a web design firm. The firm hosted clients' websites and, as such, provided technical support seven days a week. Lynn's team was responsible for staffing the technical support line over the weekend, and Lynn rotated this obligation among the various staff members who reported to her. The schedule was arranged weeks in advance, and before setting the schedule, Lynn checked with everyone to find out their preferred weekends. Weeks later, Sharon, one of Lynn's reports, approached her to discuss her rotation:

Sharon: Lynn, can I talk to you about something?

Lynn: Sure, what's up?

Sharon: I know it's my turn in the rotation to cover the support line this weekend. But I was hoping I could switch to a different week.

Lynn: What's the issue?

Sharon: I've had a tough time with my boyfriend lately. He was traveling for the last several weeks, and the distance has been a real strain. We hardly see each other, and we really need to get away this weekend and spend time together.

Lynn: If you can find someone who wants to switch, that's fine with me.

Sharon: The thing is, no one wants to switch with me. But I feel my relationship depends on this opportunity to be together this weekend. We are even talking about getting married. I think he could be the one for me, and I don't want to blow it because I was spending the weekend at my job.

Lynn: Sharon, if you raise scheduling preferences in advance, I can work around them. But at this point it's not fair for me to just arbitrarily force someone else to switch.

Sharon: I know, and I should have realized this would happen. I just didn't know how hard it would be when he was away. I'm sorry. I totally screwed this up, and I need your help. Isn't there anything you can do? Couldn't you cover for me?

Lynn (*sighing*): Fine, I guess I can cover for you this weekend myself.

Sharon: Thanks so much.

Ultimately, Lynn solved Sharon's problem, and Sharon was extremely grateful. What about Lynn? Consider the following exchange I had with her about what had transpired:

Me: How do you feel about your conversation with Sharon?

Lynn: I'm upset.

Me: Why?

Lynn: Because I feel like a sucker. I should have told her to just deal with it and find a way to balance her personal life with her professional obligations. We do things weeks in advance in our group, and I think this last-minute request was unreasonable.

Me: Why didn't you just say that?

Lynn: That's a good question. She kept saying how desperate she was, and it made me feel terrible. I get sucked into how she feels and what she needs, even though I know it's not right. I suppose I feel guilty being the boss who refuses to help. And in those situations the easiest thing for me to do is to just solve the problem rather than confront her.

Me: But then you are left feeling resentful.

Lynn: You are right. My brain knows that she is being unreasonable. But when I am in a situation like that, it's so difficult for me to reject what she is saying. It's like I feel this pressure to help her because she asked for help and really needs it, despite the fact that it's not fair to me or anyone else.

Lynn is extremely good at understanding Sharon's story, and especially Sharon's emotions. Indeed, she is so good at it that she is willing to forgo her own happiness to make Sharon happy, notwithstanding that Sharon is the one who neglected to raise the matter at the time the schedule was made. For Lynn, the problem is different from Dylan's because it is not cognitive, but emotional. She can see logically that Sharon's story is not compelling; nevertheless, she finds it monumentally difficult to resist it and assert her own point view.

If Lynn wanted to be empathetic but not overly so, she could have responded to Sharon very differently. Imagine this continuation to the conversation between Sharon and Lynn:

Sharon: I should have realized this would happen. I just didn't know how hard it would be when he was away. I'm sorry. I totally screwed this up, and I need your help. Isn't there anything you can do? Couldn't you cover for me?

Lynn: Sharon, I am honestly sorry that you are in this situation. It's hard to balance personal and professional obligations, and I would like to help. At the same time, asking me or someone else to cover for you isn't fair. We all have personal lives, myself included, and that needs to be respected. It's a balancing act for everyone. I'm sorry, but unless you can find someone who wants to switch with you, I can't help you.

Sharon: I'm really disappointed to hear that.

Lynn: I know you are, and I wish we weren't in this situation. If you can think of other ways I can make this less difficult for you, let me know. But right now the schedule is going to stay as it is.

In this exchange, Lynn is able to see both sides and feel sincere empathy for Sharon's perspective while *still* making a considered judgment that saying yes to Sharon is not warranted. But in real life, Lynn went beyond empathy; on an emotional level she felt compelled to accept Sharon's perspective and do something about it.

There is such a thing as too much of a good thing. Edward, Dylan, and Lynn, in telling the other person's story, slipped into a situation where they empathized too much. The results are a severely weakened ability to objectively and critically evaluate the other person's story and a diminished capacity to assert one's own perspective.

HOW CAN YOU TELL?

Here are some ways to tell if you are empathizing too much with the other perspective:

▷ *Do you feel resentful once the situation has been "solved"?* One way to know if you are going too far is if your solutions don't feel like compromises, but capitulations. In Lynn's case, she found a solution that satisfied her direct report, but it left Lynn feeling resentful. Shifting perspective is meant to help you come up with creative solutions that leave everyone at least somewhat satisfied. If, instead, you find that you are constantly giving in, you may be overdoing it and losing your own story.

▷ *Are people treating you objectively worse than they treat others?* People who tend to lose their own story can become magnets for exploitation. In Edward's case, he and Helen were in almost identical situations. Both had worked at the firm for a number of years; both had landed clients before. Nevertheless, Edward was consistently being treated worse than Helen was. The persistence of this gap in the quantity and quality of leads they were each receiving from their manager is a warning sign that Edward may be empathizing too much with his manager and failing to assert his own story.

▷ *Do you back down from confrontation when someone challenges you? Do you fear challenging someone you disagree with?* In Dylan's case, the building manager intimidated Dylan by arguing that "I know more than you" about the matter of market rates for rentals. Dylan was complicit in this tactic, as he quickly conceded and deferred to the manager's argument. In most stuck situations there are good arguments to be made on both sides. If you are repeatedly buying into the other side's logic without asserting your own, you may be losing your own story.

ADVICE

The goal of shifting perspective is to avoid a contest of perspectives, where one perspective is the winner and the other is the loser. Instead of thinking that it's "either my view *or* your view," you move toward thinking about "my view *and* your view." A flexible mind doesn't see just one side or the other, but holds both perspectives at the same time and doesn't feel compelled to reject one in favor of the other. Building the capacity to stand in the middle and shift between the different points of view is the ultimate goal.

Standing in the middle is difficult, though, and people stray off course. People's tendencies regarding shifting perspective exist on a continuum. At one extreme are people who tend too far toward seeing only their own story; they must work extremely hard to fight that tendency and open their minds to other points of view. At the other extreme are people who tend too far toward seeing the other side's point of view and losing their own perspective; they become easily swayed when confronted or are made to feel guilty.

Dennis and Leo are two eighth-year associates working for the same large law firm. Both were nominated for partnership this year. Following the annual partner meeting, neither one was promoted to partner. They had very different reactions to the news. Consider the following dialogue with Leo:

Me: So what do you think about the news?

Leo: I'm quite upset about it. Miles, the managing partner, was going on about how bad a year it was financially, but that is bull. Sure, they laid off a few low-performing and easily expendable first-year associates. So what? They kept all of the real workhorses—the senior associates, including me.

Me: Don't you think the bad economy is real?

Leo: It's true that the firm did not grow this year, unlike in years past. But even Miles admitted that revenues were the same as the previous year, meaning that they all made plenty of money, probably double on average compared to what I make. I think they just don't want to share the wealth and are using the bad economy as an excuse to exploit us for another year.

Me: What do you think your prospects are for next year?

Leo: I plan to look for another job and confront them with a competing offer. If they don't make me partner then, I'm leaving the firm.

Contrast that with the dialogue I had with Dennis:

Me: So what do you think about the news?

Dennis: Obviously I am disappointed. But I know it's been a difficult year economically. They did lay off a few junior people, and revenues did not go up at all compared to last year.

Me: What do you think about your prospects for next year?

Dennis: Miles, the manager partner, told me that this year was an exception, and my chances for making partner next year are excellent.

Me: Do you accept that?

Dennis: I do. I think they are generally fair. I make a good living now, as an associate. Plus, as Miles said, there are a lot of unemployed lawyers, so I guess I am lucky to have a job at all.

Two people, two different reactions to the same information. Each of them has become immersed in only one side's story. Leo is completely engrossed in his own perspective, rejecting any legitimacy to what the managing partner has to say. Dennis is at the other extreme, accepting completely and almost uncritically the managing partner's perspective, and in the process losing his own.

Each tendency has strengths and weaknesses. Leo's devotion to his own narrative creates a strong incentive to promote him next year, as the partners know how unhappy he is and may fear losing him if they don't make him a partner. However, even if he gets promoted, Leo risks damaging relationships by pushing his own story too hard. Moreover, if Leo has overestimated his worth to the firm and/or antagonizes some people along the way, they may choose to let him go rather than give in to pressure and promote him.

With someone like Dennis, on the other hand, the incentive to promote him is much weaker. Because Dennis simply accepts the partners' narrative and buries his own frustrations, there is no pressing reason to alter the status quo. Nevertheless, Dennis's ability to empathize with the firm's partners promotes and preserves goodwill, and makes it unlikely that he will antagonize or alienate the people he works for. If he does make partner eventually, he will probably not have made any enemies along the way.

Naturally, most people are somewhere in the middle. In some situations, they become like Leo and go too far toward clinging to their own point of view. In other situations, they become like Dennis and begin to lose their own point of view.

But whether the Dennis style is your dominant tendency or merely an occasional challenge, standing in the middle is the goal. Here is some advice to help you keep track of both stories, rather than giving up yours and getting sucked into the other person's narrative:

➤ *Write down each side's story.* One way to resist being swept up in the other side's narrative is to write down both stories—your side and their side. Putting the two stories side by side on a piece of paper is a tangible, physical reminder that there are multiple points of view, and that you don't need to pick one or the other just yet.

➤ *For each point, imagine the counterpoint.* When listening to the other side's narrative, conjure in your mind the opposite point. For example, when the building manager says to Dylan, "Over time you won't save time by moving," Dylan could simultaneously think, "Or, perhaps, over time I will save money by moving." When Edward is told by his manager, "Don't worry, you will get your chance," he can think, "Or, perhaps, if I don't fight for it or change this dynamic, I'll miss my chance." The goal is not necessarily to refute the point the other side makes but simply to remind yourself that there are two sides to the issue, and both sides need to be heard.

➤ *Slow down the process.* Losing one's own story often happens under pressure. Because you can't think of a response quickly, you give in to the other person's story. Slowing down gives you time to reflect and consider the issue from all angles. In Lynn's case, Sharon's intense feelings created an urgent pressure on Lynn (at least in her mind) to say yes to Sharon's request. Slowing down can relieve the pressure. If Lynn were to say to Sharon, "I have to think about it; I'll let you know later today," she might have avoided giving in when she didn't want to. She could have at least found a compromise that would have left her feeling less resentful.

▶ *Get help.* If you are susceptible to being swept up in the other side's story, either because saying no is hard for you to do or because you feel you lack information and expertise, get help from someone you trust. Ask a friend to tell you if you are going overboard empathizing with your counterpart and losing your own story in a way that is hasty or unfair. But choose your adviser carefully; if you pick people who are blindly loyal to your side, they may take a maximalist position and declare any concessions you make to be "giving in." Ideally you want to ask someone with enough distance from your situation to give you an objective and honest assessment.

HAVING THE CONVERSATION

Let's return to Edward, the investment banker who felt passed over time and time again by his boss, Maurice. Imagine that Edward has reflected on his dynamic with Maurice and now realizes that he needs to assert his own story more forcefully. How can he reengage with Maurice in a more productive manner?

The goal for Edward is the same as for the various other protagonists described in this book—to have a conversation in which various perspectives can be discussed and in which the parties can collaborate on finding a way to get unstuck. The difference is that most people need to *decrease* their emphasis on their own perspective; Edward, in contrast, needs to *increase* it.

The general advice for Edward is to find a way to toggle between the two perspectives. That is, in the conversation with Maurice, Edward should move back and forth between their respective points of view. Doing so shows respect for Maurice's perspective while making room for Edward to disagree and offer a contrary view. Because Edward tends toward deferring to the other side's point of view, toggling is a way to give expression to that instinct without letting it take over the entire dialogue. Here are some concrete tips that can help Edward (and anyone with his tendency):

▷ *Begin by describing the other side's perspective.* This is a good way to start the conversation, as it demonstrates that Edward has heard and understood Maurice's point of view. Moreover, it gives Maurice a chance to correct any misperceptions that may exist.

▷ *Ask if the other side is ready for you to share your own perspective.* This signals a transition in the conversation, where Edward will begin to offer his view. While it may be framed as asking for "permission," the deeper purpose is to help Maurice get mentally ready to hear a contrary perspective without getting defensive.

▷ *Don't shy away from confronting your differences head-on.* For people who tend to empathize too much, this may be the hardest part. It is important for Edward to be direct and clear about his differences with Maurice, and not give in to the tendency to minimize or hide disagreements.

▷ *Acknowledge the other side's contrary view even as you assert your own view.* Along the way, as Edward shares his own view, he should make references to Maurice's perspective, acknowledging that Maurice likely disagrees. Doing so demonstrates that Edward understands that there is a gap in perspective, which he would like to bridge. By modeling his own awareness of and openness to considering both sides, Edward helps Maurice do likewise.

▷ *Express empathy for the other side's position.* Maurice may find it difficult to listen to Edward. It's unusual for Edward to confront Maurice in this way—so some empathy will help Maurice adjust to this "new" kind of conversation. Empathy and acknowledgment along the way also help Maurice resist his own urge to interrupt and contradict Edward, or to mentally shut down and stop listening to Edward.

▷ *Maintain openness.* Precisely because people such as Edward don't have these kinds of conversations often, what often happens is that they overcorrect and lose their ability to hear the other side at all. In Edward's case, his frustrations pour out and are intensified by his determination to tell his own story. To have a truly productive conversation, Edward needs to walk a fine line—sharing his story while remaining open to any new data Maurice may share.

If Edward were to perfectly execute all of the advice described (something unlikely to occur in real life), a follow-up conversation with Maurice might sound something like this:

Edward: Maurice, I want to talk about this most recent sales lead that was assigned to Helen, and about how leads are divided between me and Helen more generally.

Maurice: Okay.

Edward: To summarize what you told me so far, I understand that you assigned this particular lead to Helen because you believe she is in the best position to close the business. This decision is based partly on her having a bit more experience than me, as well as you judging that her style will work better with this client. Is that correct?

Maurice: Yes.

Edward: And you feel it is your job as the manager to look out for the firm's interest, rather than any individual salesperson's interest, which is why you gave the lead to her.

Maurice: That's right.

Edward: Finally, you said this particular client represents a big opportunity, and if I were to screw it up it would look quite bad for me, and you don't want my reputation to suffer as a result.

Maurice: Right. Helen has more of a track record, so one lost prospect wouldn't hurt her as much as it would hurt you.

Edward: I understand. Is it okay if I share my own thoughts on this topic?

Maurice: Sure.

Edward: First of all, I believe you have a biased view of my skills because you have not had a chance to see me in action. For a while now you have been giving Helen the best leads; that helps her to continue closing more business than me and that, in turn, leads to her getting more leads, and so on. It is a cycle that builds on itself. I think you don't realize how much more I can do for this firm if given a chance.

Maurice: Well, Helen is a proven success, and I go with the people I know can get the job done. That's only natural, isn't it?

Edward: It certainly is natural. Given your sense of Helen's skills, compared to me, an unknown quantity, I totally understand why you've acted as you have. In fact, it's what I think many people would do in the same situation. But the problem is that you are only operating based on the information you have and not doing things to gather new information about my skills. I've been on your team for two years, and you haven't really given me a chance.

Maurice: Hmm.

Edward: I would even say I think your current approach underutilizes the team. Helen has more leads and more clients to follow up on than I do. If you balanced the workload and gave me some of the leads, I would have more time to devote to them than she does.

Maurice: That is an interesting point. But what if you don't close the business? That would look very bad for you. And I don't want to take a chance with the firm's best leads.

Edward: I understand what you are saying, and I know it feels risky. As the head of the team and the one who gets the leads and assigns them, you are personally responsible for making sure we close enough business each year. That makes sense. And I would be happy to talk to you about ways to manage that risk.

Maurice: Good. Listen, Edward, I think you have potential, but you are not as seasoned as Helen. You have some blind spots that need work.

Edward: I'd like to get your feedback. If there are specific ways you think I could improve, or if you have a problem with how I interact with clients, please let me know. Everyone can get better, and I am no exception. I would welcome your input.

Maurice: Sounds good.

Edward: I'd also like to take issue with something that I see happening on the team. I don't think it's reasonable to have two direct reports with the same job who are treated so differently.

Maurice: What do you mean?

Edward: If you think I am unqualified and want to fire me, that's one thing. But if that's not the case, then just having me hang around to pick up the scraps while Helen gets all the choicest leads is not only unfair; it's not in the firm's interest. I will never improve as a salesperson and make my biggest contribution if you don't give me a chance. I can't hit the ball if you don't let me get up to the plate and swing a few times. Sure, I might strike out, but so can anyone. I will never become a clutch hitter if I just sit on the bench or get to the plate in low-stakes situations. You are my manager as well as hers, and you owe me the chance to play.

Maurice: So where does that leave us?

Edward: Well, there is one more point I want to mention. I was very disappointed when you gave this most recent lead to Helen, since I felt we had made an agreement that it would go to me. Now, perhaps I misunderstood what we agreed. Did you have a different understanding?

Maurice: Yes and no. I did plan to give you the next big lead, but when this one came in, I thought it was a little too big to take a chance on. I'm sorry if that made you upset.

Edward: It did upset me, but I understand your reasoning. You felt that this was too big an opportunity to experiment with. Is that right?

Maurice: Yes.

Edward: For me, the problem is that it could happen again. That is, we might make other agreements regarding leads, and a similar thing happens and you have a change of heart and then don't follow through on what we agreed. That is hard for me, because then I can't know what to expect. Even when you say you will do something, I still don't know if you will follow through. And it is precisely the really juicy leads that I need you to give me, at least sometimes, so that I can prove myself to you.

Maurice: I take your point.

Edward: So, I would like to make a plan for how you can give me more good leads—really good ones, where there is something at stake—so that you can find out what I can do. I won't let you down, but you can't find that out unless you give me a chance.

As you can see, Edward was deliberate in laying out Maurice's perspective before sharing his own, one of the keys to having a constructive dialogue. In addition, he did not shy away from confronting their differences head-on, being careful to always acknowledge Maurice's contrary view as he asserted his own. Contrast this with the earlier conversation, in which Edward allowed Maurice to establish his story without too much contradiction. While he may have picked at the details, the overall narrative was Maurice's. Here, Edward toggled between their respective narratives, allowing the two narratives to be heard side by side. Toggling between their stories (e.g., "I am sure you think X, while I believe Y") is a way to stand in the middle and hold on to both sides at the same time.

SUMMARY

Flexing one's mind and shifting perspective is analogous to correcting one's vision. Both myopic (nearsighted) and hyperopic (farsighted) eyes need corrective lenses to achieve 20/20 vision. However, the way these lenses work to correct eyesight—namely, the way in which light rays pass through the lens—is different. Myopic lenses decrease how much the light bends to allow one's vision to focus properly. Hyperopic lenses increase how much the light bends to allow vision to focus properly. The lenses work in directly opposite ways, but the end result of perfectly focused vision is nonetheless identical in either case.

The population of eyeglass wearers, however, is not divided fifty/fifty between these two groups. A much larger percentage of people are nearsighted, which means that most of the eyeglasses in the world are made to decrease the bend of light. At the same time, a small but significant portion of the population is farsighted. For them, glasses that decrease the bend of light would only make their vision worse. Their correction is to compensate in the opposite way.

For the majority of people in most stuck situations, the most common problem is seeing only their own perspective. The journey to a flexible mind moves from their own view outward, toward telling their story first, then looking from the outside in, then seeing the system. And as a result, most of this book offers advice on how to make those shifts.

Nevertheless, there is another group of people in stuck situations that have the opposite tendency. They also fail to see multiple perspectives, but not because their minds are closed. On the contrary, they are so open they are swept up in the other side's narrative and tend to lose their own in the process. It may happen when they feel a lack of confidence on the cognitive level, or when they are emotionally hooked by the topic.

To face the challenge of seeing the other side's point of view while simultaneously remaining true to your own story, you need to take concrete steps to toggle between perspectives. Whether empathizing too easily with other people and losing yourself is your dominant tendency or only an occasional struggle for you, keep in mind that your goal is always balance—finding a way to stand in the middle and see both sides, not just yours or just theirs.

Learning to toggle between your perspective and the different viewpoints you've now acquired requires practice. The next chapter examines techniques for role-playing that can be enormously helpful in diagnosing where you are at and planning your next steps for getting unstuck.

CHAPTER **8**

Practice, Practice, Practice

GETTING TO CARNEGIE HALL

"*I need* help in being more assertive," said Liz, a new coaching client. "I try to be firm, but somehow I always find myself giving in when colleagues ask me to work on their projects." I asked Liz to try practicing saying no by role-playing with me. I would play her colleague asking for help, while Liz would simply be herself and try to say no.

Me (as colleague): Liz, can you help me on the XYZ project?

Liz: I'm really busy.

Me (as colleague): But I know you can do a great job. Without your help, I'll never get this done.

Liz: I don't know . . .

Me (as colleague): Please say yes. I'm counting on you.

Liz: Well, I'll see if I can free up some time.

I paused in the role play and asked Liz how she thought it went. "You're just like my colleagues," she said. "Even when I say no, you get me to say yes."

I pointed out, "Liz, you never said the word *no*." Liz replied, "I thought I did say no. I felt I was saying no clearly." We reviewed the short conversation again, and Liz was stunned when she realized she never said the actual word "no." And she admitted she needed practice to get better at saying no.

We role-played again and again, and I kept asking Liz to be as firm as she could, making sure to actually say no to her colleague. Finally, after several tries, she managed to utter a gentle no.

Role-playing is an extremely powerful technique for improving your communication skills. It can help you to diagnose your problem in a stuck situation and practice better ways to respond. Through role-playing a conversation she found difficult, Liz discovered that she hadn't actually been saying no to her colleagues and, in the process, was able to try out a different way to respond. I have used role-playing both in training groups and in one-on-one coaching to help my clients become more self-aware and to improve their skills. But to make good use of this phenomenal tool, one needs to first understand what role-playing is and how to do it.

WHAT IS ROLE-PLAYING?

The other day I was watching my sons, ages six and four, acting out a scene with a bunch of stuffed animals. The scene they had invented had both good guys and bad guys, with dialogue between the various characters. It was fascinating to watch them practice their use of language and imagine how the conflict between the good guys and bad guys would get played out.

As adults, we don't usually engage in "pretend" conversations; that's something we leave behind as we get older. When we talk to each other as grown-ups, we are discussing real things in "real life." Nevertheless, having a conversation that is pretend can be a useful learning tool for adults, just as it is for children.

We can practice things to say, and we can identify and understand our own feelings, just as children do, by exploring them in a pretend conversation—a role play.

Before I go into depth on how to role-play and how it can help you, let's dispel a common misconception. People often mistakenly believe role-playing is a form of acting. And it's easy to see why this misconception arises.

Actors, after all, are grown-ups engaged in a pretend conversation. Actors follow a script and create an impression in viewers' minds in order to entertain and stimulate the audience. Even though we know that the conversations are pretend, good acting makes them look very real. The best actors seem to inhabit their characters and to become the roles they play onscreen or onstage.

Indeed, I once watched an interview with an actor who plays a charismatic head of a crime family in a television series. This crime boss is beloved by fans, and the actor said that sometimes when he goes out people will treat him as they would treat the character he plays—with deference, respect, and awe. And in the interview he said, "This is just a character I play—he is a criminal. That's not me. It would be awful if I started to think that the character is real and who I really am."

Part of what makes acting seem so real is the tightly managed, prewritten script that breathes life into a scene. Although role-playing to an extent allows you to orchestrate what to say in advance, there are real differences between acting and role-playing.

Role-playing is a pretend conversation in which each person is assigned a particular character in a conversation. However, there is no script to follow. Within their respective roles, each person tries to be his genuine self, letting his true reactions and feelings guide the action. If what happens in the role play makes him feel angry, then his character will become angry. If what happens makes her feel nervous, then her character will become nervous. The role player is not deciding in advance to feel angry or nervous, the way an actor would in accordance with the directions of the script and the director. Role players are *spontaneously and authentically* feeling angry or nervous in their role. The unscripted nature of role-playing, in which the actual dynamic between the parties drives the conversation forward, allows the conversation to go anywhere. This often leads to dialogue that neither party expected and opens a window into what is "going wrong" for the person in a stuck situation.

An example will highlight how acting and role-playing differ. Imagine that you need to have a tough conversation with your boss in which you are going to ask for a raise. You are nervous about the request and how your boss will react. You would like to practice the conversation, so you'll feel more comfortable and confident when you have the opportunity to speak with your boss. And you have a choice—you can act out the conversation or you can role-play the conversation.

If you chose to act out the conversation, you would write a script that included your lines and your boss's lines. You would find an actor to play your boss. A good actor would ask you about your boss and try to adopt his style of speaking and mannerisms, in order to give a good performance. You would both learn your lines and seek to make the conversation as realistic as possible, with dramatic pauses, appropriate facial expressions, and so on. Depending on what you predicted would happen, you would write a script that would have your boss accepting your request or rejecting it, or perhaps putting up a fight and finally relenting. You would rehearse with your friend until you had mastered the performance of your pretend conversation. At that point, you would go and have the real-life conversation with your boss.

Acting out a conversation can have value. Practicing lines to say is helpful, and thinking about how you want to frame your request for a raise is smart. Moreover, in creating the script, you are already anticipating what your boss is likely to say and thinking about how to counter it.

On the other hand, the problem with having a script is that the other side might deviate from it. What if your boss doesn't respond the way you expect? What if your boss goes off script? Not only are you left unprepared, but you may become flustered and frustrated that your boss is not following your plan. (Indeed, when one actor flubs his lines, the other actors can become confused since the entire performance depends on everyone saying their lines correctly.)

Contrast this with a role play. If you chose to role-play the conversation, you would do some similar things. You'd find a friend to play your boss. This friend would learn about the situation and ask some questions about your boss—to understand his likely way of thinking and feeling, rather than his mannerisms. You wouldn't have a script, though. You'd simply have an understanding of the issue (a pay increase) and the two characters (you and your boss). Once both you and your friend were ready, you would role-play the conversation. You would ask for the raise as skillfully as you could, and your friend would react in real time, in whatever way felt natural to him as the boss. The conversation would take on a life of its own and be driven by what you said, what he said, and your reactions to each other.

Rather than prepare for a specific response by your boss, you would prepare for many different possible responses. Indeed, you might role-play a few different versions of the conversation, gauging your friend/boss's reaction each time, as you looked for the best way to make your case. You might also think about your own feelings; as you interacted, where did you get upset? Which parts of the conversation made you most nervous and uncomfortable? After doing this for a while, you would not have memorized a script of the conversation at all. Rather, you would be armed with some insight into your own feelings, some guesses as to what your boss might say in response, and some ideas for where the conversation might go.

What's most important and useful about role-playing is that

it is a pretend conversation where the feelings and reactions are *real*. The context is created artificially—that is, in this example, your friend is only pretending to be your boss; he's not your actual boss. But how he reacts to you is how your friend, playing his character, actually feels like reacting to you. And how you react to your friend/boss is how you really feel like reacting. This authenticity is at the core of why role-playing as a learning tool works. And it can be employed in a few different ways.

ROLE-PLAYING TO DIAGNOSE THE PROBLEM

We know which conversations are challenging for us, but we don't always know why those particular conversations are the ones that make us crazy. Understanding the underlying cause —the *why*—rather than just the symptoms is a key to getting unstuck.

A client named Eve came to me for coaching when she had a difficult relationship with one of her colleagues, a man named Phil. I asked her what was difficult about her interaction with Phil, and she said, "I don't know. I guess I just don't like him. Somehow interacting with him is very tough."

To help Eve, we needed to define the problem at its core. Eve herself couldn't tell me what it was about Phil that made it so difficult for her to communicate with him. I suggested that we role-play her conversation with Phil in order to gain more insight into her challenging dynamic with him. Here is how I prepared her:

Me: So, let's play out a conversation between you and Phil. You will play yourself, and I will play Phil.

Eve: Okay.

Me: In order for me to play Phil, I need a little background about your situation. What is the issue you are discussing in this conversation?

Eve: Phil and I are peers. We both are senior research analysts at an investment firm, and we both report to the portfolio manager. One issue we fight about is getting research analysts assigned to our investment ideas. Both Phil and I come up with possible investments for the portfolio. But once the idea takes shape, there is a fairly lengthy process of doing background research to test the idea and see if it can withstand scrutiny. There is a team of junior analysts available to us to help do the background work, and Phil and I often fight about getting these analysts assigned to our respective ideas. The portfolio manager is fairly hands-off and lets us come to these decisions more or less on our own.

Me: So essentially you are arguing that the analysts should be assigned to you, and he is arguing that the analysts should be assigned to him.

Eve: Basically, yes. I think things should be divided more equally, whereas he will say his investments have a better track record, which is why his ideas should get precedence, which I think is not true.

Me: Let's set the stage, then. Where would this conversation take place?

Eve: In a conference room at our office, where we would have privacy.

Me: When would it take place?

Eve: Probably at the end of the day, after the market closes.

First, I needed to understand enough of the context and the substantive issues between Eve and Phil so that I could role-play in a realistic way. At a minimum, I needed to understand what we were talking about and what was at stake—the who, what, when, where, and why of the situation. But to fully delve into the role of Phil, I needed more information.

Me: Okay, so that is the context, which I think I understand. Now, for me to play Phil authentically, I need to know a bit about him. What is he like? What is his style of communication?

Eve: Well, he is friendly to everyone most of the time, but he can also become pretty aggressive. He is quite nice at first, but then turns nasty and puts you down. He is not above making a hurtful comment if it will help him get what he wants.

Me: So, friendly, but turning to aggressive when I don't get what I want?

Eve: Exactly.

Me: Is there anything else you want to tell me about Phil to help me get into his character?

Eve: No, I think that's it.

My goal in this role-play was not going to be solving Eve's problem. I simply wanted to diagnose what made interacting with Phil so difficult for Eve, so she could develop an understanding of why she struggled.

In order to re-create the negative response that Phil triggered in Eve, I had to play Phil authentically. And that required getting a sense of Phil's style and patterns. I asked Eve for some input, but I added things that I envisioned Phil would feel based on my ability to tell his story. Since Phil was not present to share it, I needed to imagine stepping into his shoes, recognizing the various things noted in Chapter Five: In his story, Phil is the hero. In his story, Eve is the villain. In his story, his intentions are good. And so on.

At this point we were ready to proceed. Here is the conversation we had, with me playing Phil and Eve playing herself:

Me (as Phil): Eve, you wanted to talk to me?

Eve: Yes. I have a new investment idea and I want to get one of the analysts to help me research it.

Me (as Phil): I think that's great. I'm happy to chat with you about it if you want.

Eve: Well, I think I have the basic idea; I just need one of the analysts to dig into the numbers.

Me (as Phil): Look, everyone is already assigned to other projects. But you can research this on your own.

Eve: But, Phil, all three analysts are working on your investments. They are supposed to be a shared resource. I need some help.

Me (as Phil): Eve, that's because my ideas are the most promising investments right now. The idea is to make as much money as possible for the fund. Why aren't you being a team player?

Eve: I am being a team player.

Me (as Phil): Eve, we both know that your ideas have been pretty weak lately. You get an idea and want to start spending time and energy pursuing it before you've fully done your homework.

Eve: I disagree.

Me (as Phil): Did you have a big loser recently?

Eve: Yes, but that wasn't my fault. All of my other ideas have made money.

Me (as Phil): Do you really want to go head-to-head with me in front of the portfolio manager? I don't think that would go well for you.

Eve: Well . . .

Me (as Phil): You need to prove yourself. Until then, I don't think you have a lot of right to be demanding more resources for your ideas. Research analysts go to people who can make money for the firm.

Eve: (*Silence.*)

Now I needed to discuss the conversation with Eve:

Me: Was this conversation close to how things would go in real life? Did I play Phil in a realistic way?

Eve: Absolutely.

Me: So, how did you feel during the conversation?

Eve: Exactly like I do in real life.

Me: Which is how?

Eve: Uncomfortable. Nervous. Like I just wanted the conversation to be over.

Me: I sensed that you felt uncomfortable. Do you remember when those feelings first kicked in?

Eve: I don't know. I think it was when you challenged me to go head-to-head in front of the portfolio manager.

Me: How did you feel in that moment?

Eve: It made me feel insecure, like maybe you were right, maybe my ideas were not that good. And so I started to back down and basically stopped fighting with you.

Me: I think that's right. When Phil challenges you openly, that's when you shut down. And he pushes your buttons by suggesting you are not good at picking investments.

Eve: You are right. He does that a lot, and while I could not define it before, that is the dynamic we get into.

Me: And as Phil, I felt your hesitation. That made me suspect you are not that confident about this new idea anyway, since you were not willing to fight me for it. Moreover, I felt emboldened to challenge you openly, since I sensed you would back down if I became more belligerent.

Eve's example demonstrates how role-playing, done right, re-creates not just the words of the real-life conversation, but the emotions as well. Eve started to feel the way she felt in real life—a sure sign that the conversation was quite authentic.

The feelings I felt playing Phil were also relevant. I sensed weakness in Eve, and as Phil, I wanted to push her harder to get what I wanted. I suspected that the real-life Phil might feel the same way.

In this example, role-playing was used to *diagnose* what made a conversation difficult. It helped Eve become more aware of her own reactions and which of her buttons were being pushed. This self-awareness, in turn, would help Eve manage her reactions in the future and explore alternative ways to respond to Phil and people like him.

ROLE-PLAYING TO LOOK FROM THE OUTSIDE IN

Seeing oneself from the outside is hard to do. Role-playing, combined with a video camera, can break through a person's resistance and raise your awareness of how you are truly perceived by others.

Alphonse was a senior partner in a consulting firm. Known for his technical expertise, Alphonse was also infamous for chewing out employees who made a mistake. Clients loved Alphonse, because he did excellent work. Staff was a different story. Senior managers would rotate onto Alphonse's team to get some experience, but they seldom stayed more than a few months. Even successful staff members would flee Alphonse's team because of the stress of working for him.

The firm's executive committee told Alphonse that his manner of handling employees was hurting the firm and limiting his own success. They asked Alphonse to work on his management skills, but he denied that there was a problem. When I was asked to coach Alphonse, I realized the first step was to break through the resistance and show Alphonse how he looked from the outside. Here was our initial conversation:

Me: Alphonse, what do you think of the feedback you've gotten?
Alphonse: I think it's overblown.

Me: What do you mean?

Alphonse: I don't think I am that harsh when I deal with employees. Naturally, if employees make a mistake I will let them know, but I am perfectly willing to hear their side of the story. I think people need to be more assertive.

Me: Why don't we role-play a conversation in which an employee made a mistake, to see how it goes?

Alphonse: Okay.

Me: And if you don't mind, I'm going to videotape it, so that you can see how you come across and judge for yourself.

Alphonse: No problem.

At this point, Alphonse identified a situation with an employee named Rick that would be good to role-play. Rick was a senior manager who reported directly to Alphonse. Rick was a talented consultant, and Alphonse thought he might make partner at the firm if he continued on his current track.

In the situation in question, Rick had been staffed on a large client engagement. As is the case with any engagement, the scope of the work that the firm committed to perform, and that the client committed to pay for, was clearly described. However, while working on the engagement, Rick identified some new tasks that needed to be completed, but that were outside the scope of the contract. Thus, the client's willingness to pay for the out-of-scope work, and the fee associated with that work, needed to be negotiated. Rather than raising the issue with either Alphonse or the client, Rick went ahead and did the work on his own. Only when the assignment was completed, and Rick's timesheets were submitted, did the out-of-scope work come to light. Alphonse was furious at Rick, and the feedback session did not go well at all. It was this feedback conversation that we role-played:

Alphonse: Rick, you screwed this up completely.

Me (as Rick): Hold on a second, you don't know the context . . .

Alphonse (*interrupting*): I don't give a crap about the context. You needed to raise this issue. How could you fail to do that?

Me (as Rick): I was totally focused on getting everything done on time, and I just didn't have an opportunity to raise it.

Alphonse (*yelling*): That's absurd! You could have e-mailed me or called me.

Me (as Rick): But you are not available, and that would have delayed things. And anyway, it's not something I could easily put into an e-mail. This client is touchy about fees, and I didn't want to antagonize them.

Alphonse: There is absolutely no excuse for failing to raise the issue. This is a rookie mistake. How am I supposed to negotiate with the client over a fee for your work when they never agreed to it? How could you be so stupid?

Me (as Rick): (*Silence.*)

Alphonse: I just don't understand how you expect to make partner with these kinds of mistakes.

We paused here, and I stopped the recording. I then played back for Alphonse the video of the conversation and asked for his reactions:

Alphonse: Wow, that was eye-opening.

Me: What did you notice?

Alphonse: Well, I was furious, and for good reason. But I never let Rick talk.

Me: I think you are right.

Alphonse: I just shouted over him. At the time I thought we were having a dialogue, but I can see that it was quite one-sided.

Me: Do you think this kind of dynamic happens in other situations where you get upset with direct reports?

Alphonse: I'm not sure. But I think I need to find out.

In this case, role-playing helped Alphonse open up to seeing himself from the outside in. From here, the coaching continued with an exploration of how Alphonse tended to react when he was angry and his struggles with listening when he was sure he was right. When I tried discussing these matters with Alphonse before the role play, he was totally closed to what I was saying. But seeing himself on the video shattered his defenses and opened him up in a way that mere discussion and analysis could not.

ROLE-PLAYING TO TELL THEIR STORY

The experiential dimension of role-playing also makes it a powerful tool in learning to tell the other person's story. Sometimes, merely asking someone to consider the other person's point of view, as described in Chapter Four, does not succeed in opening his mind and unlocking his communication skills. When just thinking and reflecting on the situation isn't enough, role-playing is an effective way to break through resistance.

Harvey worked at an agriculture company. He was a successful sales representative and had been promoted to territory manager. It was in the role of manager that Harvey began to struggle. He had received feedback that he was too aggressive and too demanding with his direct reports. I was asked to coach Harvey and help him become more skilled in managing people. Our session started when I discussed with Harvey what he thought the problem was:

Me: Your employees say that you are aggressive and demanding.

Harvey: I'm just trying to get them to do their jobs.

Me: They've also said that you micromanage them and want to control how they get their work done.

Harvey: Those are excuses. Their sales numbers are not good enough, and if they would follow some of my advice, they would do better. How do you think I got to be a manager? By being a fantastic sales representative. If I tell people to make more cold calls or to visit more prospects, I have a good reason for it. People are lazy and don't want to do the hard work of selling.

Clearly, Harvey was steeped in his own point of view. The best way to get Harvey to see his subordinates' point of view—to tell their story—was to have him role-play with me. This time I recommended a role reversal and asked Harvey to play the role of one of his direct reports. I needed Harvey to truly take on the role of a person who reports to him, something he had resisted doing thus far, so that he could see the other side's point of view.

Enrolling in someone else's character can be quite easy, but when you detest that person's point of view, it's very challenging. If you hate your mother-in-law, you would be uncomfortable enrolling yourself in her character. It isn't fun to make her the hero, turn yourself into the villain, and assume her intentions are good. Nevertheless, it is precisely with the people you most detest that the need for understanding is greatest. If you don't get into their shoes, how will you understand their point of view? And if you can't understand their point of view, how will you be effective in unlocking your stuck dynamic with them?

Once I explained my reasoning to Harvey, he finally agreed to proceed. He said that he was having a particularly difficult time managing an employee named Walt. Thus, I needed to make sure Harvey really got into Walt's character before we could have the conversation.

For a short while, Harvey was going to become Walt. He

would work to take on Walt's persona and perspective as authentically and sympathetically as possible. I set things up as follows:

Me: What is your name?

Harvey: My subordinate's name is Walt.

Me: I understand that. But right now, I want you to *become* Walt. So, answer in the first person. What is your name?

Harvey (as Walt): My name is Walt.

Me: What do you do for a living?

Harvey (as Walt): I sell agricultural products.

Me: How long have you been doing this job?

Harvey (as Walt): About five years.

Me: Are you good at it?

Harvey (as Walt): I think I am. I know my customers and my territory.

Me: Who is your manager?

Harvey (as Walt): His name is Harvey.

Me: What do you think of Harvey?

Harvey (as Walt): He is fine, I guess.

Me: Is he pushy?

Harvey (as Walt): Yes. He can be a real jerk. He is always telling me how I need to have more contact with my customers.

Me: And what do you think?

Harvey (as Walt): I think he needs to leave me alone.

Me: What do you mean?

Here Harvey paused. I could see that he was reflecting on what he would feel and think if he were Walt. His answers came more slowly as he struggled to get into Walt's head and imagine how Walt would react.

Harvey (as Walt): I know my job, and I do it differently than he does.

Me: Have you tried to tell him that?

Harvey (as Walt): Yes, I have tried.

Me: And what happened?

Harvey (as Walt): He doesn't want to hear it.

Me: What does he say?

Harvey (as Walt): He says, "You are wrong; you will sell more if you do it my way."

Me: Is he right?

Harvey (as Walt): I don't know. (*Pausing.*) But either way it's annoying that he won't listen to me. He doesn't show me respect, so I shut out what he's saying.

At this point Harvey was ready to enter into dialogue, with me playing Harvey and him playing Walt. Our conversation went as follows:

Me (as Harvey): Walt, you need to go visit your clients more often.

Harvey (as Walt): Look, I have visited every customer at least once this season. They are busy planting right now—it's not the time to pay a visit.

Me (as Harvey): Well, I'm telling you that now *is* the time to do it. That's how I've been so successful as a sales representative—by getting out there and seeing my clients as often as possible.

Harvey (as Walt): Maybe that's your style, but it's not mine.

Me (as Harvey): I think it should be.

Harvey (as Walt): I need to do things my own way. Stop micromanaging me.

Me (as Harvey): Walt, if you are not going to make more sales calls, we're going to have a problem.

At this point, I stopped the role play and, together with Harvey, analyzed the situation. Here was our debriefing conversation:

Me: So, what did that feel like?

Harvey: That was strange.

Me: Why?

Harvey: Well, once I started really getting into Walt's character, I got mad at Harvey.

Me: What made you mad?

Harvey: His boss doesn't give him any respect. He just tells him that he is wrong all the time, and doesn't listen to a word he is saying. He just wants things done his way. And I, as Walt, didn't like to be controlled like that.

Me: What else?

Harvey: Well, I recognized that the things you said—when you were playing me—were things I had said myself in real life. And when I said them as me, they seemed totally reasonable. But as Walt, they pissed me off. It felt very aggressive, and kind of disrespectful.

Me: So, with both stories now in your mind, are there changes you would make in how you deal with Walt?

Harvey: I still think Walt does need to call his customers more often. Although I understand his point of view and his feelings much better, I don't think he is right. So what do I do now?

Me: Getting to the point you are at right now—being able to understand Walt's perspective and feelings, even though you still disagree with him—is more than half the battle. Now your job is to show Walt that you understand, so that you can open his mind to hearing your point of view.

Getting unstuck is what this book is all about. And it starts with flexing one's own mind to see things from multiple perspectives. So far, role-playing had helped Harvey flex his mind. He was now ready to take the next step and practice having a different kind of conversation with Walt in the near future. And here, role-playing can again be helpful.

ROLE-PLAYING TO PRACTICE

As mentioned already, role-playing is not acting. There is no script to memorize, and the assumption is that the other side may react in a variety of ways. Nevertheless, just as actors rehearse, role-playing can be used to practice skills and improve one's ability to react well in a conversation.

Harvey acknowledged that his earlier conversations with Walt and other employees had gone badly; he understood that in the past he was not able to tell their story. To have a constructive conversation, Harvey would have to engage with Walt differently. In Chapter Four we discussed the importance of summarizing and acknowledging the other side's point of view in order to shift the conversation. In Harvey's case, the key was for him to show that he *understood* Walt, without necessarily *agreeing* with Walt, so that they could explore together their differing perspectives on selling. While Harvey, as manager, had the power to tell Walt, "Do it this way because I said so," this approach wouldn't generate much enthusiasm or commitment to doing things differently. Until Walt felt that his view had been heard, and until his feelings were addressed, he would be fighting against Harvey's point of view, rather than being open to it.

"But how do I do that?" Harvey asked. I explained that we would role-play again, only this time Harvey would play himself, and I would play Walt. Harvey's job was to have a constructive conversation, summarizing and acknowledging Walt's perspective. Here was the conversation:

Harvey: Walt, I want to talk to you about how to get your sales numbers up.

Me (as Walt): Okay.

Harvey: I think you need to call your customers much more frequently. That is the key to making more sales.

Me (as Walt): I can't do that. I don't want to pester my customers.

Harvey: Give my strategy a chance. It's not pestering them—it's your job to stay in touch with them.

Me (as Walt): I call on them when I think I need to. No one likes pushy salespeople who are constantly trying to move product. Let me do my job my way.

Harvey: I know you think that, but I honestly believe you are missing out this way.

Me (as Walt): I know my territory, and it won't work.

Harvey: I'm sure you disagree with me, but this truly is a better way. Please give it a try. I know you can do it.

Me (as Walt): (*Silence.*)

At this point, we ended the role play and I again debriefed Harvey:

Me: So how did that go?

Harvey: Not that great. It wasn't that different from before. I don't know why.

Me: Well, what were you trying to do?

Harvey: I was trying to use the insights I gained from our earlier role play. I understand Walt's reluctance to call on customers, but he needs to do it if he wants to improve. I also understand that he doesn't like being micromanaged and told how to sell. But at the same time, it's my job to get his sales numbers to go up. I don't know how to get him to see the light.

Me: I think the problem is that, while you have a better understanding of Walt's point of view now, you did not let that show in the conversation. You just told him your point of view over and over.

Harvey: That's not accurate. I said to him "I know you think that" and "I'm sure you disagree." Doesn't that show I understand his point of view? The problem is that his point of view is wrong!

Before I go on, please consider your own response to Harvey's question. Did Harvey show that he understood Walt's point of view? If you were Walt, would you feel understood if someone said those things to you?

My answer to these questions is no. Simply telling people, "I know you disagree," does not demonstrate that you understand what they think, why they think it, or how they feel. Walt has no way of knowing if Harvey understands his point of view.

Even saying "I am sorry you feel that way" still doesn't show you understand the other person's point of view, although it's perhaps a polite and caring thing to say. You are expressing sadness that the person holds that point of view—but did you really grasp the other point of view? Were you able to tell the other person's story?

The best way to show that you understand the other person's point of view is to summarize it. State your understanding of the point of view so that the other person can see you really do get it. And I needed to get Harvey to this next step:

Me: Well, I don't think you showed Walt that you were able to tell his story. You can say "I know you disagree" as many times as you want, but that still doesn't prove to Walt that you heard him.

Harvey: Then what will?

Me: Here's an idea: Why don't you summarize what you understand Walt's position to be?

Harvey: You mean to agree with him?

Me: No. Just tell him your understanding of his story. And if you don't completely understand his story, ask him some questions to clarify.

Harvey: But won't that annoy him?

Me: I highly doubt that. Let's give it a try.

We then did another role play, with Harvey trying to practice explicitly showing Walt that he understood his point of view:

Harvey: Walt, I want to talk to you about how to get your sales numbers up.

Me (as Walt): Okay.

Harvey: I think you need to call your customers much more frequently. That is the key to making more sales.

Me (as Walt): I can't do that. I don't want to pester my customers.

Harvey: I want to make sure I understand what you are saying. You are uncomfortable calling customers because you feel that would be pestering them?

Me (as Walt): Yes. And I resent you telling me how to handle my customers. I know my territory, and it won't work. People don't like a hard sales pitch. It's too aggressive.

Harvey: I'm hearing you say two things: One is that you don't want to be aggressive with customers and bother them, and the other is that you feel I am micromanaging you and telling you how to do your job.

Me (as Walt): Yes, that's right.

Harvey: Okay. How often do you call on customers now?

Me (as Walt): Usually once at the beginning of the season, and once again in the middle of the season. Beyond that I'm mostly reacting to customers who call me.

Harvey: So, is there a way you could speak to your customers more frequently that would not feel pushy or aggressive?

Me (as Walt): I don't see how. If I am not calling on them to sell something, why am I calling on them?

PRACTICE, PRACTICE, PRACTICE

PRACTICE, PRACTICE, PRACTICE 221

Harvey: Well, there are a lot of ways to make a customer call without pushing a product. Sure, you want to make a sale eventually, but talking to customers can also be a way to learn more about their needs, understand their fears, and generally deepen your relationship with them so that they will think of you first when they do need to buy something.

Me (as Walt): Hmm. Can I do that without being pushy? I don't want to damage my customer relationships. Not only are these the people that buy my product, but many of them are people from my community. I don't want to offend them or get a bad reputation.

Harvey: I understand your concern about protecting relationships. You need to find a way to call on customers that feels right to you and won't antagonize them.

Me (as Walt): Exactly!

Harvey: So, let's talk about a way to balance that concern with my concern. My fear is that if you don't talk to your customers more often, you will miss out on sales opportunities. Can we try to achieve both of these goals?

Me (as Walt): Maybe. How would that work?

This version of Harvey's conversation with Walt was much more collaborative and constructive, and it's worth exploring why.

For Harvey to bridge the gap between himself and Walt, he had to find a way to bring both perspectives—his and Walt's—into the dialogue. Walt was clinging to his own point of view, and resistant to Harvey's coaching, particularly because it was delivered in an aggressive manner. As with many psychological defenses that people adopt, the more you confront them, the more strongly they push back. Harvey's goal was not to defeat Walt, but to defuse him. And the way to disarm Walt is to acknowledge and respect his point of view. Harvey can do this concretely, by summarizing what Walt says to convey that he understands.

It is essential to keep in mind that just because Harvey can summarize Walt's point of view, that does not mean he agrees with Walt's point of view. People often struggle with this distinction: Listening isn't the same as agreeing. Just because you let people share their point of view, take time to consider it, and even summarize to show you understand it, does not mean you agree with it.

CREATING YOUR OWN ROLE PLAY

You don't need to hire a professional coach in order to role-play; it is a method that anyone can use on a stuck situation. Here are a few simple steps to help you make use of this powerful tool.

Step One: Find a Partner

Finding the right partner to role-play with is important. You want that partner to be someone you trust. Why? Because role-playing requires both sides to relax into their roles and to allow themselves to truly experience whatever emotions emerge from the situation. Role-playing may take one or both people outside of their comfort zone, or reveal underlying issues that are usually kept hidden. The power of role-playing comes from its authenticity, and that authenticity requires vulnerability. Therefore, trust is the most important ingredient in choosing a role-play partner.

It is also helpful to choose someone who is not too deeply familiar with the situation. One element of a successful role play is allowing people to react to one another in a genuine way. If you choose someone who already knows the situation and the

PRACTICE, PRACTICE, PRACTICE

individuals involved, chances are that person is going to bring biases and preconceptions to the role-played conversation, and that's the *opposite* of what you need. You are looking for someone who will react authentically in the moment, not someone who will replay a tape of what has been said in the past or automatically inject preconceptions into the dialogue.

For example, imagine that I have a challenging dynamic with Oliver, a manager in the operations department at my company. Whenever I ask Oliver for help on something, he gives me a dozen reasons why he can't help me. Although his job is to provide operational support to our group, he is unresponsive to our team's requests for help. Things have gotten to the point where I, and all of the people on my team, do everything possible to avoid dealing with Oliver because he is so annoying.

I'd like to make things better, and want to role-play a conversation with Oliver to prepare for a real conversation I plan to have with him. I think about choosing Cal, one of my teammates who has also had run-ins with Oliver, to role-play with me. But Cal is likely to play Oliver the way he experiences Oliver—that is, as a difficult, annoying, and lazy person. Because Cal is so familiar with the situation and has his own story about it, he won't play Oliver as Oliver would; in fact, he'll probably play Oliver as he appears in Cal's story—without even realizing he is doing so. This is the problem of nested unawareness (described in Chapter Four). Cal won't tell Oliver's story because he is too deeply inside his own story.

What I actually need is an outsider—someone who is sufficiently removed from the situation that he can play Oliver in a sympathetic and humanizing way, and then respond in the moment to what happens during our role play. An outsider who doesn't know Oliver, or at least doesn't know him well, will not have biases to resist. This outsider might be someone from another department, or even someone not from work, but rather a friend or family member.

Step Two: Set the Stage

Once you've chosen a trusted partner who is able to engage in role-playing without being overcome by his own biases, you need to set the stage. Setting the stage has two parts: 1) describing the substantive context and 2) describing the dynamic of the interaction.

The substantive context refers to the "facts of the case." It's an exploration of the "who, what, when, where, and why" of the situation. It is not necessary to explain every detail of the substantive context, but your role-play partner needs to know enough of the context to be able to respond to your questions or comments. In particular, your partner needs to know enough to be able to tell the story of the person he's role-playing—in this case, Oliver. If my role-play partner is my brother, I need my brother to know enough about the company and how our team interacts with the operations department to tell Oliver's story. Remember that this is distinct from telling *my* story about Oliver. This is telling *Oliver's* story about himself.

To make sure your role-play partner knows enough about the character to play that person accurately, start by answering the following questions:

- What is this person's job?
- Who does he report to?
- Who are his clients or customers?
- What are his responsibilities?
- What are his goals?
- What pressures does he face in doing his job?
- What are sources of tension or frustration for him in his job?

▸ What challenges does he face in getting his job done well and on time?

Your role-play partner also needs a chance to ask questions of his own about the role he's playing. For example, if my brother needs to play Oliver, he may ask, "What is preventing Oliver from simply saying yes when you ask for something?" It is easy for him to think of this kind of direct question because he's trying to get into Oliver's shoes and has a better sense than you do of what is missing in the other side's story. If you find you cannot answer questions your role-play partner asks about the situation or about your counterpart, it is usually a sign that you don't fully understand the other side's story. It may also indicate what topics you should be exploring once you are in the conversation.

In addition to the facts of the case, you need to inform your partner about the dynamic of your real-life conversations. This is the "how" of the conversation, as opposed to the "what." Ideally role-play partners will be able to capture not just the content of what their character thinks and says, but also the attitude and style with which they say it. Why is this important? Because the "how" of your situation may be the essence of what makes it challenging. If your partner can find a way to re-create that, it may open your eyes to seeing what is getting you stuck. In the example of Eve, as described previously in this chapter, Phil's aggressive style was as much the problem as his assertion that his investment ideas should take precedence over Eve's. My role-playing of Phil in an aggressive way led Eve to a greater understanding of what was holding her back. The closer your partner can bring you to experiencing your real-life counterpart, the greater the insights you will glean.

Here are some questions to help your role-play partner capture the style of the other person:

- What is this person like?

- What is her communication pattern?

- Is the person passive or aggressive?

- Is she loud or quiet?

- Is this person direct or indirect in how she expresses herself?

- Does she speak quickly or slowly?

- Is she deliberate or impulsive?

- Does this person tend to interrupt or wait until the other person has finished before speaking up?

Naturally, your answers to these questions—that is, your description of your real-life counterpart—will be somewhat biased. Don't worry too much about it. I didn't know whether Phil was as pushy and aggressive as Eve claimed he was, but I was able to play Phil the way Eve experienced him and re-create for her how it feels when he pushes her.

Also, don't worry if your partner is not perfect at capturing how your real-life counterpart talks. In many ways the "how" is created by the "what," and if your role-play partner is successful in telling the other person's story (which, for an outsider, should not be that difficult), he will be able to communicate in a fashion that is reasonably close in its essence, if not in all the details. I could figure out enough about Walt's story from Harvey's (biased) description of him to know that Walt was frustrated and even angry, so I role-played Walt as frustrated and angry in the conversation, even though Harvey never told me to. Of course, people express frustration and anger in many different ways, and I may not have captured the way Walt would have expressed these feelings. Nevertheless, the emotions were accurate, and Harvey was able to learn by engaging with my character's frustration and anger.

Step Three: Have the Conversation

Once the stage has been set, have the conversation with your role-play partner. You don't need to talk at length—five minutes is probably enough. Indeed, it's worthwhile *not* to go too long, because if you do, you are likely to forget what happened at the beginning of the conversation. A few minutes of honest dialogue that gets at the heart of the issue is probably enough.

Your job is to simply be yourself and engage with the other side. You should pay attention to what you are experiencing as the conversation progresses. Here is a sample dialogue between me and a partner role-playing Oliver:

Me: Oliver, I want to talk to you about finding meeting space for our upcoming conference. It's not that far away and we need to find a nice space.

Partner (as Oliver): I have more urgent things that need handling right now. I can't work on your conference that is six months away.

Me: But if we wait, we may be locked out of all the best locations.

Partner (as Oliver): I just don't have time. You will have to wait. I have other clients.

Me: I can't believe that you won't even start looking now. It's not that big a deal—why can't you work on more than one thing at a time?

If your partner plays his character in a completely unrealistic fashion—too aggressive or not aggressive enough, too loud or not loud enough, etc.—you can pause and offer some more guidance or refinements on how your real-life counterpart actually communicates. I have often asked my clients if I am playing their real-life counterpart authentically, and if not, I solicit feedback and adjust accordingly. A bit of fine-tuning can make the role play far more productive, so don't be shy about giving a little direction.

Step Four: Stop and Debrief

After the role play has progressed for a few minutes, it's time to stop the action and reflect on the conversation you just had. Here are some key questions to consider:

> How did I feel during the conversation?

> Did anything surprise me in this conversation?

> What did I like/dislike about how I handled the conversation?

> What would I do differently in a real conversation?

Immediately following a role play, your partner is in a unique position to give you feedback, too, as he has just had an authentic experience interacting with you. There is, of course, no guarantee that your role-play partner's experience will be the same as your real-life counterpart's. Nevertheless, this feedback can give you a very good guess as to what the person might be experiencing. Here are some questions you should ask your role-playing partner:

> How did you feel during the conversation?

> What impact did my words and comments have on you?

> What did I say that was most helpful? What did I say that was least helpful?

> What do you think I could have done differently?

Imagine that I paused the role play with Oliver and asked my partner, "How did you feel, as Oliver, during this conversation?" Consider the following feedback conversation:

Me: So, what did you think? How did the conversation go for you, as Oliver?

Partner: Well, you were very aggressive.

Me: What do you mean?

Partner: You kept trying to get him to do what you wanted. I have to admit that, although I am your friend in real life, you made me feel pretty defensive as Oliver. You need to give the guy some credit for trying to do his job well, and ask him some questions about what he has going on—you just went on the attack!

This is challenging feedback. It is hard to give and hard to receive, but exceptionally valuable. In most of your stuck situations, you will get feedback that is difficult to digest, and that's why a strong relationship with your role-play partner is so important. It would be unfortunate if my response to my partner's feedback would be to get defensive and burrow even deeper into my own story. Learning and growing in stuck situations requires that we be vulnerable, which is why working with a trusted role-play partner is so important.

During debriefing, you can also share your own reaction to the role play and ask your role-play partner for advice:

Me: It's so frustrating dealing with Oliver, because no matter what I say he always has an excuse.

Partner: I think your frustration is showing, and it comes across as aggressive.

Me: But I don't know what to do instead.

Partner: You could try explaining your frustration. Or you might try asking questions and getting Oliver to open up and explain how he balances the needs of his various internal clients.

Me: I'd be willing to give that a try.

Step Five: Try Again

Once you've done the role play and analyzed it, take advantage of the opportunity to try it again, incorporating the feedback you just received. In this case, the second round of role-playing, which incorporates feedback received from Oliver's perspective, might sound like this:

Me: Oliver, I want to talk to you about finding meeting space for our upcoming conference. We need to find a nice space; the conference is not that far off.

Partner (as Oliver): I have more urgent things that need handling right now. I can't work on your conference that is six months away.

Me: Can you tell me about some of the other things you are working on?

Partner (as Oliver): Sure. I have a conference coming up in two weeks for Allan, and I have a year-end report that needs to be edited and vetted by the end of the month, and I have an event for our top-twenty clients that the CEO is speaking at which I need to plan.

Me: So, you have events that are happening in the immediate future, and those take precedence. And as a result, you don't have any time to devote to my request.

Partner (as Oliver): That's exactly right. I'm sorry, but that is my situation.

Me: I understand what you are saying. At the same time, my fear is that if we don't start looking at venues for our conference now, we will be locked out.

Partner (as Oliver): Well, I am extremely busy right now.

Me: I understand that you have many other urgent priorities right now. And at the same time, I don't want to miss out by not acting in a timely fashion. Maybe there is a middle ground. Can we set a timetable for when you and I could start planning? That way I won't have to bother you and I can have some sense of when we will start. In addition, if you could give me a sense of the budget I will have to work with, then I could do a little research and see what's available now. What do you think?

Partner (as Oliver): I'm happy for us to speak at the end of next week. I'll e-mail you a rough budget, based on last year's conference, but beyond that I can't spend any time on this until next week. I'm sorry, but I just am too busy.

Me: That's fine. Getting the budget and meeting next week is a good start. Thanks.

Don't be surprised if you need to practice several times before you get to a conversation you feel comfortable with. Flexing one's mind and changing one's communication patterns are hard work. You may also experiment with different approaches to the conversation before deciding on which one would work best.

As you role-play, you will notice a process of first becoming aware of what is happening in the conversation—your words, your feelings, and the other person's reactions. As your awareness grows, you can begin a process of changing the conversation—saying different things, managing your reactions better, and responding more skillfully to the objections of the other side.

Role-playing will also help you communicate your message in your own style. In training a newly hired employee on how to teach a workshop on communication skills, I invited the employee to listen to my presentation. When it came time for him make the presentation, it fell flat. Why? Because he tried to copy what he had seen, even using my jokes and comic pauses. That is a recipe for failure. To communicate with maximum effectiveness, we need to find our own way to share our point of view. While inspiration and advice can come from others, you have to find a way to express yourself that is authentic and honest. Role-playing allows you to practice doing just that.

SUMMARY

The power of shifting perspective is a major theme of this book, and Chapters Four, Five, and Six offer specific ways to flex one's mind. Yet thinking and analysis, whether done alone or with another person, are sometimes not enough to unlock one's mind and allow other perspectives in. Role-playing is a behavioral tool that will help you progress. It is an active and experiential method of accessing and changing your thinking. Role-playing allows you to engage in concrete dialogue and through the live interaction explore your stuck situation from multiple angles.

Role-playing also improves your communication skills. It helps you execute constructive behaviors and move from thinking to action. The practice of asking questions and summarizing another person's perspective will help you engage in these behaviors when confronted with challenging situations in real life.

It is fascinating to me how quickly people's minds can change just by having a short role-played conversation. Whether it's by playing yourself and soliciting honest feedback on how you sound, or stepping into the other person's shoes and seeing how the conversation looks from there, role-playing is a real eye-opener.

Now that you have practiced, it's time to use what you have learned in your role play to decide what action to take in your particular stuck situation. Making change happen is the topic of the next chapter.

What Comes Next

MAKING CHANGE HAPPEN AND
IDENTIFYING DEAD ENDS

AB $Fashions$ was a four-year-old startup company founded by Alice and Barney. The idea for the online clothing firm came from Alice, who brought with her several years of fashion design experience. She met Barney while they both were working for an established clothing company, where Barney led a production team. Both partners were excited to start their own business, and their respective skills and experience in design and production were highly complementary. They decided to leave the firm where they worked and launch AB Fashions as fifty/fifty partners.

Things started out fine. They both worked hard, and the company slowly but surely built up a base of customers. But about two and a half years after they began working together, Alice and Barney's relationship became strained. They began fighting over almost every decision. A typical encounter went something like this:

Alice: Barney, I am really unhappy with the suppliers you picked for the spring designs. I saw the samples we received, and I think the quality control needs to be more rigorous. Going forward I need to be included in your conversations with suppliers.

Barney: Hold on a second, Alice. When we started this business it was understood that production decisions would be my area of responsibility and authority.

Alice: Since then things have changed. I have more experience than I did before, and I have a lot of opinions about production.

Barney: I'm happy to hear your thoughts, but I don't want to wait for your approval for everything I do. I don't try to control what you do with the designs.

Alice: I need to have a say in production, Barney. I just do.

Barney: Why are you trying to control the production process?

Alice: I'm not trying to control it. But with all due respect to your expertise, I have a lot to contribute in that area. And this is as much my company as it is yours.

Barney: This is not what we agreed to.

Alice: We are fifty/fifty partners, remember?

Barney: Why are you micromanaging me?

Alice: You need to act like a partner, who makes decisions with me, not like my boss. Stop trying to control everything!

They began avoiding each other, each making decisions without consultation whenever possible, just to avoid fighting. Although the company was successful, neither one of them was happy. Moreover, their tense dynamic posed a threat to the future of the business.

Alice was uncertain about what to do. When she tried to discuss things with Barney, their conversations devolved into arguments, going nowhere. The company was profitable, and Alice enjoyed her design work, but her desire for more participation in production was left unsatisfied. At the same time, she knew that many of her friends had jobs that were far less satisfying. Leaving the business was an option, but that was bound to be a painful and expensive process and not something she wanted to rush into. Alice was certain that she needed to try everything before making the decision to leave.

Alice was in a classic stuck situation. As we learned in the preceding chapters, in order for Alice to change things, she should flex her mind and shift perspective, considering the situation from other points of view. She should take a moment to consider how Barney would describe things. She also ought to consider her own blind spots. And, finally, she should consider how the overall structure of the situation (in this case, the company and the role of each principal) is contributing to the challenging dynamic.

This chapter addresses what comes next. Assume that Alice successfully flexes her mind and shifts perspective—then what? How do things progress? Alice's case will illustrate three different possibilities for how stuck situations can get resolved. Shifting perspective is key for applying any of these three options—and for deciding which is right for your stuck situation.

POSSIBILITY 1: THE SITUATION GETS BETTER AND THE RELATIONSHIP IMPROVES

Suppose that, after flexing her mind, Alice comes to a number of realizations. Having considered Barney's story, she understands that, for him, her push to participate in production feels like interference and micromanagement. Barney has spent years working with suppliers overseas, carefully building relationships, and getting to know each one's strengths and weaknesses. Because of his years of experience as well as his network of relationships, Barney indeed believes he knows more than Alice does about the production process. Alice's demand for equal decision-making authority in this area is not only frustrating, but in Barney's mind, it has the potential to undermine the success of the business. He feels entitled to deference in his area of expertise.

In addition, Alice realizes that her own, direct style clashes with Barney's more indirect style. She knows, after having role-played with a close confidante, that Barney likely thinks she is demanding an equal vote in decision making for production, rather than asking to be a part of the process. Although it was not her intention, that is how she was understood. How she is phrasing her request is as much a problem for Barney as the content of what she is saying.

Finally, Alice reflects on the fact that as a company, she and her partner hadn't done much to articulate areas of authority or define a decision-making process. At first the company was so small and had so few customers that it hardly mattered; they were in constant communication and collaborated on every decision. Over time, however, as their business grew, the lack of structure became a weakness leading to these tensions.

Having succeeded in telling Barney's story, looking from the outside in, and taking into account the system, Alice would be empowered to improve their relationship. She could then approach Barney again and have a new conversation:

Alice: Barney, I want to talk to you about the production issues I raised earlier.

Barney: Fine.

Alice: Before getting into the issues, let me say that I realize that I may come across as pushy, and that was not my intention. I want to talk this through, but sometimes my style makes it seem like I am not open to discussion. So if you felt that way, I apologize.

Barney: I appreciate you saying that.

Alice: I also want to say that I tried putting myself in your shoes.

When I did that and reflected on the situation, I thought that you might experience my desire to get involved in production as micromanagement. Am I right?

Barney: Sort of. It feels like you don't trust me, which is galling. After all, you know how much experience I have in production. Don't you think I am doing a good job?

Alice: In general I do, although I have some concerns. But I am inferring that it's not just the interference that bothers you, but the implicit message that I don't trust you or rely on you to handle things. Is that right?

Barney: Yes.

Alice: Okay. I understand that, and I am sorry that it came across that way. I also think that, in the absence of any specific agreements about who is responsible for what in our firm, it's easy for these kinds of disagreements to erupt. Beyond this one issue, perhaps we should spend time mapping out responsibilities more generally.

Barney: That is probably a good idea.

Alice: Do you feel like I have understood your concerns?

Barney: I think so.

Alice: Good. So, I'd like to tell you why I want to be involved in production, and see if we can find a way to compromise.

Barney: Okay, shoot.

As can be seen in the dialogue, Alice's shift in perspective allows her to be much more empathetic to Barney and makes her a much better listener. By telling Barney's story, she realizes that he feels his expertise in production is essential to the success of their business. By being willing to see herself as he sees her, Alice can acknowledge that the way she has broached the topic thus far is difficult for him. By looking at the system, Alice recognizes that the lack of structure and clearly defined roles and expectations is contributing to her frustration. Alice incorporated these lessons into her new conversation with Barney, and the conversation that took place following her shift in perspective was far more constructive than the original conversation had been. Together, Alice and Barney may now find a number of solutions to their problem. For instance:

> Barney updates Alice weekly on various production issues.

> Alice shares her opinion about production, but Barney has the final say.

> Only production decisions that have a major impact on the appearance of the garment require Alice's agreement.

> Alice will engage Barney in her design process, creating balance and reducing Barney's feeling of micromanagement.

> Barney will introduce Alice to suppliers so that she can have input, but Barney will remain the primary point of contact on any production issues the suppliers need resolved.

Alice and Barney's situation, as described here, is an example of the situation becoming unstuck because the parties are able to have a better conversation and thereby create options. Most of the examples in the previous chapters follow this path. Change yourself, change how you think and how you interact, and things can be transformed.

But that doesn't always happen. Sometimes, even flexing one's mind is not enough. Imagine that, although their conversation is more constructive, Alice and Barney continue to fight about her involvement in the production process. Then what?

POSSIBILITY 2: MAKING PEACE WITH THE STATUS QUO

Another possibility is for Alice to unilaterally change her own attitude about the situation. Thus far, Alice has been focused on making the situation different. She wants to participate in the production process and is trying to find a way to satisfy that desire. What if Alice were to accept that Barney needs autonomy in production? She might decide that, although it is frustrating, the overall relationship is worth more to her than this one issue, and therefore she is willing to defer to Barney's needs on this topic.

It's important to understand that making peace is not the same thing as giving up. Giving up is resigning yourself to a situation that you do not truly accept but feel powerless to change; as a result, you passively submit to the situation. Making peace is an active choice to accept the current situation and to sincerely let go of the desire to make it different.

Consider the following example. Dahlia was frustrated by her babysitter, Betty. She had been working with Dahlia for four months, and Dahlia's kids adored her. This was no small thing, as Dahlia's kids were energetic and required a skilled and experienced babysitter to handle them. Betty loved the children as well, and they always seemed happy to see her. Dahlia, who had a somewhat flexible schedule but nonetheless worked full-time, had to juggle her professional and family obligations, and so she depended on Betty.

The problem was that Betty was quite disorganized. She would ask for a day off at the last minute, throwing Dahlia's schedule into disarray. She would sometimes bring the kids home from the park late without calling to let Dahlia know, creating anxiety. When Dahlia raised her concerns with Betty, Betty would shut down, exiting the conversation as quickly as possible. The atmosphere between Dahlia and Betty became increasingly tense, and as Dahlia's frustration grew she considered replacing Betty. While grappling with the question of whether to fire Betty, Dahlia came to me, and we had the following conversation:

Me: Why are you considering firing your babysitter?

Dahlia: Because she is driving me crazy.

Me: What is she doing that drives you crazy?

Dahlia: It is lots of little things. For example, she will ask me for a day off at the last minute because she forgot to tell me that her mother is coming to town to visit, or because she neglected to tell me that she scheduled an appointment. I've told her a million times to give me notice, even just a day or two in advance, and taking time off won't be a problem, but she doesn't.

Me: What else?

Dahlia: She always comes to work on time, but she will take the kids out and come back late. I've asked her to call me if she is coming back late, but she often forgets her cell phone, making her unreachable. Or, she takes it, but leaves it on vibrate and doesn't hear me calling.

Me: Why do you think she acts this way?

Dahlia: She doesn't respect me as her employer. If my boss told me to schedule my days off in advance, I would make sure I did that. It's true that the kids love her, but I don't have to be treated this way.

Dahlia saw Betty's behavior as inconsiderate and disrespectful of her employer's time. In that frame of mind, it was understandable that Dahlia wanted to terminate Betty.

However, it was also clear that Dahlia was not telling Betty's story the way Betty would herself. In Dahlia's narrative, Betty was disrespectful. This perspective made it hard for Dahlia to feel anything other than anger and frustration. Considering how Betty would describe her own behavior, however, could open up other possibilities.

I continued my conversation with Dahlia as follows:

Me: Let's try to tell Betty's story the way she would. If she were in this room, what would she say?

Dahlia: She would probably say that she can't help it; she just loses track of time. She would also say that she does respect me, and she's sorry for the last-minute requests for time off.

Me: And what do you think of that?

Dahlia: I would say that the words are nice, but if she really cared she would be more organized.

Me: Do you see her being organized in other areas of her life?

Dahlia: No, not really. In fact, I know she isn't organized, because she often does things like pay her rent late, for which her landlord charges her a late fee. It's not a lot of money, but it's a total waste. You know, she also forgets things at our house, like her phone charger. She is pretty disorganized in general, not just in relation to her job with me.

Me: Given that, here is another way to frame what is happening: Betty is not being disrespectful to you; she is in fact giving you her best. But her best is flawed.

Dahlia: That is still very frustrating.

Me: I'm sure it is. I would feel the same way you do. But ask yourself this: How is Betty as a babysitter otherwise?

Dahlia: Except for these issues, she is fantastic. My kids adore her and are excited to see her. She loves my kids and knows how to handle them. She is fun, and warm, and full of energy. Truth be told, it's not easy to find a babysitter that can handle my boys, but she can.

Me: So, Betty is a great babysitter in so many ways, but she has these annoying weaknesses. Is that a fair assessment?

Dahlia: Yes.

Me: Here is how I see it: If you take her disorganized behavior person-ally, it will enrage you. But if you reframe this circumstance in your mind, you can see she is not doing it to you as an individual; she just behaves that way in general. And then the question is, Can you make peace with Betty being this way, and accept these flaws as part of an overall package that is actually a great babysitter for you? Or would you prefer to fire her and look for someone else who would be more organized?

Dahlia: I have to think about that.

Dahlia subsequently noted that the shift in perspective was hugely helpful to her. It did not alter Betty's behavior at all, but it transformed how Dahlia thought and felt about Betty's behavior. And she realized that since no babysitter is perfect, she would prefer a disorganized babysitter who loved her kids to an organized babysitter who loved them less. Dahlia still wished Betty were more organized, but she decided to stop trying to make Betty different and just made peace with her being a wonderful, but flawed, employee.

In considering whether making peace with the status quo is something you should do, try applying a cost-benefit analysis. Ask yourself:

- What aspects of this situation are making me unhappy?
- What aspects of this situation am I satisfied with?
- How does my current situation compare with what I might find if I left the situation?
- Is it worth it to me to live with the difficult aspects of the situation, considering the positive dimensions to this relationship?

If your answer to this last question is yes, you can make peace with the status quo.

Acceptance as a Catalyst for Change

Paradoxically, *accepting* the current situation as it is has tremendous potential for changing the situation, beginning with making an internal change in how one person feels. Dahlia understands that Betty simply doesn't know how to be less disorganized, and therefore Dahlia experiences far less frustration and resentment toward her babysitter. Alice is accepting of Barney's need for autonomy and makes peace with it in the context of their overall business relationship. This is the first change.

But the transformative potential of making peace goes beyond one person's internal experience. Once that person feels differently, she is likely to interact differently. The more Alice pressures Barney to let her participate in production, the more he resists. Once Alice can genuinely accept that Barney needs autonomy and let go, she is likely to be gentler and more empathetic in how she communicates with him. These subtle changes in their dynamic can, over time, influence the other side's behavior as well. Barney may feel less threatened by Alice and gradually open up, over time including her more in the production process.

Indeed, the simple fact of the acceptance is something your counterpart is likely to detect. Dahlia's acceptance of Betty and her flaws is something that Betty will probably pick up on. When Betty senses that Dahlia has let go of trying to make her be different, Betty may take the initiative to examine her behavior and work on her weaknesses on her own. Remember, Betty's disorganized behavior is not something she is proud of, but something she struggles with. When Betty is busy defending her ego from Dahlia's criticisms, she is less likely to change. But if she feels accepted by Dahlia, she might try to change on her own. In Barney's case, once Alice lets go he is free to, on his own, examine his reaction and explore whether he might be able to include Alice in some of his areas of responsibility without feeling micromanaged by her.

Nevertheless, it is pointless to accept the status quo while harboring a secret hope or expectation that this "acceptance" will ultimately facilitate the other person changing on his own. Not only is this risky, as your counterpart may never change in the way you hope, but that secret hope is likely to seep through and be felt by the other side, nullifying the acceptance you were purporting to show in the first place.

In trying to sincerely accept the status quo, something to keep in mind is that making peace is an *active* choice. There will be times when that acceptance is tested. In those moments of frustration, which are inevitable, remind yourself that you made a conscious decision to make peace with the situation, believing it was the right course of action; it wasn't imposed on you. Recalling that it is a choice can be comforting, as it reminds you that you are an active partner to your relationship, not a victim. Maintaining an active rather than passive mindset is helpful both in making peace and in walking away, as will be described next.

POSSIBILITY 3: WALKING AWAY

This possibility is, in many ways, the hardest one for me to write about. I've just spent eight chapters urging you to resist the voice in your head that says this situation or problem is hopeless, and to try to make things better by being different yourself. I've argued that if you change your own thinking as I have described, you can be different, and the whole dynamic can shift.

Nevertheless, some situations can't be fixed. There are dynamics doomed to stay stuck, in which changing yourself just won't work. And making peace won't work either, as the negatives of the current situation outweigh the positives, making the status quo unsustainable. As disappointing as that is, it's important to know when to call it quits and move on. How do you ascertain when it is time to walk away?

HAVE YOU REALLY TRIED?

Before walking away, you need to make sure that you have tried to shift perspective in an authentic way. While this chapter is predicated on the assumption that you have already succeeded in shifting perspective, it's important to revisit this assumption, as one of the subtle ways people resist flexing their minds is by claiming that they already have.

I once taught a workshop on listening skills. Listening to other people can influence them to listen to you in turn. In contrast, not listening to the other side makes it much more likely that other people will refuse to listen to you.

A participant in the workshop named Janie said, "My boss won't listen to me. I am a great listener and listen attentively to him, but he doesn't ever want to give me a turn. What can I do?" Suspecting that there was more to the story than Janie described, I invited her to role-play her conversation with her boss. I would play the boss, and she would play herself. She gave me a bit of the background, and we had the following role-played conversation:

Me (as boss): Janie, we need to cut your budget.

Janie: We can't do that.

Me (as boss): Look, I know you have already made cuts this year, but . . .

Janie (*interrupting*): You don't understand. If we cut any more we will have to shut down several programs.

Me (as boss): Janie, we need to . . .

Janie (*interrupting again*): I know what you are going to say—that we don't have the funds to support all the programs. But the cuts you are proposing don't work.

Me (as boss): Can I tell you what senior management is saying right now?

Janie: You can, but I've heard it before. It doesn't matter what they say, it won't change the reality. We are making a big mistake.

Following the role play, I asked Janie if this was a typical conversation between her and her boss, and she said that it was eerily similar to real life.

You be the judge: Was Janie listening well? I think not. All she did was interrupt. What is even more interesting than how poorly Janie listened was how she *thought* she had listened well. Indeed, her question in the workshop was predicated on her having listened endlessly to her boss while he refused to give her a turn to speak—the opposite of what actually happened. And Janie was not being manipulative or deceptive. She sincerely believed that she had listened well.

You may recall the concept of "nested unawareness" described in Chapter Four, in which not only are we unaware of how to tell the other side's story as they would themselves, but we are unaware that we are unaware. We believe we have successfully told their story when we have not.

Let's expand this phenomenon to shifting perspective in general: We all are at risk for claiming we have flexed our minds when, in truth, we have not. This matters, because if we merely think we have flexed our minds but haven't, we may give up prematurely and walk away from situations that could have been resolved. And for that reason, if things are not getting better, give yourself one more try at seeing other points of view before calling it quits.

Check Yourself

To make sure you are not quitting prematurely, try answering questions that deal with each of the three shifts in perspective described in this book. Here are some questions to help you do a thorough job:

Tell Their Story

> Have I put others at the center of the narrative?
> Have I made them the hero?
> Have I attributed virtuous intentions to their actions?
> Have I made myself the villain?

Look from the Outside In

▷ Have I acknowledged my own contribution to this negative dynamic?

▷ Have I seen how my behavior is reflective of my own flaws?

▷ Have I identified my blind spots in this situation?

▷ Have I gotten feedback about my behavior from people I trust?

See the System

▷ Have I taken the time to consider how the structure of the situation is getting in the way or making things worse?

▷ Have I identified the nonpersonal, systemic dimensions to our stuck situation?

▷ Have I examined the impact of our respective roles on our interactions?

▷ Have I explored the role other parties may be playing in this conflict?

If you are able to answer these questions in the affirmative, then you've likely done a good job flexing your mind. If you still feel stuck, and your conversations aren't making things better, and if you aren't sure whether you want to or can make peace with the situation, it may be time to go.

TIME TO ACT

Once you've actually shifted perspective, it's time to decide. The choice is between making peace or walking away. The common thread is that, in either case, you are making an *active decision* about what to do.

I once was hired by a small firm that was struggling to achieve its goals. The head of the firm asked me to interview all of the employees to determine what was wrong and to offer recommendations on what to do about it. This was a "superhero" type of organization, where nearly everyone reported directly to the founder and was dependent on him for their success. The interviews revealed that a great number of the employees were deeply unhappy. They did not like how the firm was run, they did not trust the founder, and in general they felt that it was a terrible place to work. I was surprised and depressed at the extent of the unhappiness, but I was also struck by another fact: Why didn't people leave? Why would people continue to work at a job they hated, knowing it was making them miserable?

This is not an isolated case. We all know people who are miserable in their job, apartment, marriage, etc., yet don't take active steps to change their situation. These people have settled into a passive, pessimistic routine where they are victims in a negative dynamic they feel powerless to change.

Flexing one's mind and shifting perspective unilaterally is an antidote to this emotional inertia. It is an active choice. Igniting the spark of action is essential for addressing a stuck situation. In the words of Theodore Roosevelt, "The best thing you can do is the right thing; the next best thing you can do is the wrong thing; the worst thing you can do is nothing."[1]

Settling into passive unhappiness is a self-fulfilling prophecy. If you decide that nothing will help, then indeed nothing will help. But if you decide to try, you've decided to act. Once you've acted, ask yourself: Is the cost-benefit of staying better or worse than the cost-benefit of leaving? Choosing to stay is an active choice, and choosing to leave is an active choice.

Leaving a situation is never easy. Leaving too soon is a problem, which I have tried to address throughout this book. However, leaving too late is a problem as well. Here is an exercise to help you get over the hump and leave (or decide that you are ready to make peace with the status quo).

Imagine that you've left the stuck dynamic, whatever it may

be. And imagine that it goes badly. If your stuck dynamic is with your boss, imagine you leave your job and you don't find another job for a long time; now you have to face the choice of unemployment and its financial consequences or working at a job outside of your field. In contemplating firing her babysitter, Dahlia should consider that it will be several weeks before she can find another worker who is warm and loving to her children, making it impossible for her to balance her family and her career. Alice can imagine breaking up her partnership with Barney and having to start over again. She should consider that it would take her a long time to establish her business with new customers.

Now ask yourself—how does that prospect make you feel? When you *visualize your worst-case scenario,* do you feel sad for having left your unhappy but stable job? Or do you feel relieved that it is behind you? Are you nervous about the future or optimistic that things will work out?

For Alice, ending her frustrating dynamic with Barney may be a relief, and the prospect of starting over on her own may be exciting. For Dahlia, cringing at the thought of not having a loving babysitter may spur her to realize that the frustrations she feels with a disorganized Betty are not as important as the positive side of employing Betty. This exercise is useful because it accesses a slightly less calculating but more emotional aspect of the decision to leave and can provide insight into what you should do. Visualizing the worst case and gauging whether that feels better to you than the status quo may help you decide whether to make peace or walk away.

Another way to help you determine if it is time to go is to *ask your counterpart.* Alice could ask Barney, "Do you think we should keep working together?" His response may help her clarify her own feelings. If he, too, wishes to part ways, then making that decision would be an amicable process, which feels productive rather than destructive.

Making the frustrating dynamic itself a topic for discussion can be liberating. Dahlia could say to Betty, "You know I feel you are a great babysitter, and at the same time there are some sources of tension between us, like when you ask for days off at the last minute. I think it's affecting the dynamic between us, which concerns me. What do you think?" If Betty balks at the idea of planning days off, or if she responds with resentment or insincerity, it can clarify to Dahlia that this situation is no longer working.

Raising the issue of the stuck dynamic is more confrontational than simply visualizing your worst-case scenario, and in that sense carries more risk. It is far easier to broach this uncomfortable topic with a partner or a subordinate as opposed to your boss. Therefore, when engaging someone who is more senior than you, you should use caution. Nevertheless, if you are truly stuck and considering leaving anyway, the risk may be worth it. Engaging directly on the stuck topic, and tuning into both the words and the attitude of your counterpart's response, can help you determine whether things can get better, whether you can make peace, or whether you truly do want to walk away.

MANAGING RISK

In some extreme situations, it's important to walk away even without having exhausted all of the options for conversation and relationship repair. If your workplace is causing you physical harm, or if you are a victim of abuse, you need to leave immediately and seek help.

I once coached an executive named Paul. He was on a one-year assignment to take over a poorly functioning factory, evaluate and dismiss all employees who were performing poorly (which unfortunately happened to be most of them), and bring in new workers to replace them. The existing employees, who were unionized, vigorously resisted and fought tooth and nail to undermine everything Paul did. The worst dynamic was with the head of the local union, who would denounce Paul publicly and in print. Paul's friends, neighbors, and relatives all read disparaging things about him in the paper, and Paul was shamed, unable to escape people talking about him at every turn. The stresses of the job weighed heavily on Paul, and his health began to deteriorate. He developed a rash and lost twenty-five pounds during the time he worked at the factory.

Six months into this assignment, Paul was truly a mess. He was trying to decide if he should stay and complete the turnaround or leave the position. He could have made things better if, in the beginning, he had interacted more skillfully with existing employees, but six months later it was a clear case where staying posed health risks and was not warranted. Paul did not need to try harder to tell the employees' story; he didn't need to look at himself from the outside in. He needed to protect his health and leave the situation.

Serious risk to the business is another extreme situation in which walking away may be the best option. Joseph was the CEO for an investment management firm headquartered in New York City but with offices in major cities around the world. Running the London office was a talented and aggressive managing director named Luke. He frequently clashed with Joseph, claiming that the London office was being treated worse than the other locations. Joseph denied this accusation, but the arguments and tension between them persisted.

The firm was preparing for an initial public offering (IPO), and as such, Joseph wanted to avoid any negative publicity about the firm for fear of undermining the deal. He asked Luke to keep their differences out of the spotlight, at least until the IPO was completed. Despite repeated requests, Luke did not change his behavior. He was outspoken about his frustrations, sharing his complaints about how the London office was being treated with both his direct reports and with the firm's clients.

The tension between Joseph and Luke became quite acute,

and they were clearly in a stuck situation. Joseph had tried to find a way to resolve their differences, but so far had been unsuccessful. How long should Joseph go on trying to fix things?

In this case, there is a risk of serious harm to the business, and there is a short and pressured timetable for making things work. It therefore makes sense for the company to protect its interests by separating from Luke. The risk of the alternative is simply too great. Since Luke refused to change his behavior for the good of the company and was putting the entire organization at risk, it made business sense for the company to stop working with Luke.

A QUESTION OF VALUES

When confronting a stuck situation that violates one of your core values, walking away is much more likely to be the right answer.

Dale, an up-and-coming sales executive for an IT company, was having a difficult time with his supervisor, Norris. Dale took the lead on several difficult projects, but Norris neglected to give him credit or note his contribution when talking with senior management. In addition, Dale felt Norris made inappropriate comments in group meetings, sometimes embarrassing Dale. When Dale raised these issues, Norris replied, "I think you are being oversensitive. That's how we joke around on the team. Don't take it personally." Dale felt stuck and wasn't sure how to change his dynamic with Norris.

This appears to be a classic situation where flexing one's mind and shifting perspective can help Dale interact more skillfully with his boss.

But what if I told you that Dale was a woman, the only female in the group, and that Dale observed that Norris did not treat the men this way? Dale had a strong feeling that gender played a big role in how she was being treated. Does that change how we see the situation? I believe it does. Legally, the situation is different: Gender discrimination is prohibited by law in the United States and many other countries. Moreover, there is a sense that the power imbalance of the gendered dynamic makes it more dangerous for Dale to try to tell Norris's story. Indeed, if Norris's story is based in part on a belief that women should be treated differently from men, this situation would be a question of values and not something we would encourage Dale to try to embrace. This would be a situation where walking away, either by escalating the issue, engaging human resources, or even leaving the job and/or getting legal advice, would make sense.

KEEPING THE DOOR OPEN

I once mediated a divorce between a young couple who had been married for only a few months. They did not have children and there was not much property to divide, although there were quite a lot of hurt feelings between the two spouses. The mediation took place over three sessions, during which time they discussed what to do with the wedding gifts and the timeline for filing the divorce with the local court. By the end of the third session, the issues had been worked out and all that remained was to document, in legal language, the agreement that had been reached. We scheduled a meeting for the following week, when both parties would come to sign the agreement. The papers would then be filed with the court and form the basis of a divorce decree.

The next week, the young couple came back to the mediation center smiling and full of good cheer. It seemed they had spent the better part of the previous week discussing their differences and why they each wanted to separate, and then decided that they did not want to get divorced after all. We ripped up the mediation settlement, and they said thank you and went on their way.

This story has stayed with me, because it suggests something about what it takes for certain stuck situations to shift. This couple clearly had the potential to work out their differences all along, but didn't. Yet something shifted once they began actually progressing through the process of getting divorced and contemplating fully what that would mean for them. What was it?

Procrastination is the avoidance of unpleasant activities by putting them off until later. A similar emotional procrastination exists when confronting stuck situations. It's unpleasant to consider the consequences of leaving, so people avoid it. For this reason, actually walking away can ignite soul-searching and perspective shifting in your counterpart. This can transform your situation, allowing you to get unstuck and find a compromise. It might also clarify that separating is really what's best.

If Alice has done everything possible to flex her mind and can't make peace with the status quo, it's time to separate from her business partner, Barney. This may come as a relief to Barney, and they can find a way to separate with minimum cost. Or, after reflecting on the situation, Barney may decide that he wants to continue working with Alice, understanding that doing so will require him to loosen up and include her even on decisions where he believes he ought to have complete autonomy. Either way, it may take Alice's authentic willingness to walk away for Barney to truly consider what he wants.

Of course, the walking away has to be real for the transformation to take place. If you are merely pretending to walk away, hoping the other party will come after you, don't be surprised if nothing changes. Indeed, the situation may get worse, as you have lost credibility. You have to be at the brink, ready to leave. Only then can you find out if the situation is salvageable.

SUMMARY

This chapter explored the mechanics of the changes that can take place once you've shifted perspective. In the best case, you can repair a relationship and find a compromise that unlocks your stuck situation. Alternatively, flexing your mind may help you experience your stuck situation differently, enabling you to make peace with the status quo. Making peace itself can help the situation shift, as it subtly alters your dynamic with the other side in small but important ways. Finally, recognize that some situations are not fixable, and if you have truly tried everything, it is time to walk away.

My hope is that, when faced with a stuck situation, flexing your mind will help you move from a mindset of passivity and resignation toward a mindset of taking action and moving forward, regardless of the final outcome.

Conclusion

I was coaching a woman named Kara who was struggling with a particularly difficult stuck situation. She needed to give negative feedback to Marty, one of her direct reports, but could not figure out how to do it in a way that was both honest and constructive. Every time she practiced, she either came off as too harsh and negative or too timid.

I invited Kara to do a role reversal, where I would play her and she would play Marty. In the role play, I applied many of the techniques from this book, including telling Marty's story, looking at myself (as Kara) from the outside in, and recognizing the systemic conflict inherent in the power imbalance in this conversation. I toggled between perspectives and acknowledged Marty's perspective while sharing (as Kara) my own.

Kara found the role play to be extremely enlightening and resolved to apply some of the techniques in her real-life conversation. She then added, "It was amazing watching you handle Marty. You are such a skilled communicator; I bet you *never* get stuck."

That remark made me laugh out loud because of course I get stuck; who doesn't?

I'm reminded of the story I heard from an old friend about a martial arts master who wanted to teach his class an important lesson. He invited several of his students to attack him simultaneously and to try to knock him down. Punches and kicks flew, yet the teacher was able to deflect and evade all of their blows, never once losing his footing.

After this amazing demonstration, the teacher asked the students what they learned. One raised his hand and said, "I think I have discovered your secret, teacher. You were so effective in handling our attacks because you never once lost your balance." To which the teacher replied, "On the contrary, I lose my balance all the time. What you saw just now was something else—I have learned how to regain my balance extremely quickly, and that is what lets me keep my footing."

Similarly, readers of this book won't acquire magical communication powers that shield them from ever getting stuck. What they will obtain are the tools to help prevent stuck situations from occurring frequently and for handling those situations when they do arise. So, as you try to apply the skills you've learned in this book, be sure to remember these points:

➤ *We all get stuck sometimes.* If your hope was that this book would be a vaccine or antidote to stuck situations, I'm sorry to disappoint you. Getting stuck is inevitable. No matter how self-aware and skilled you are, there are going to be situations and relationships and dynamics that you struggle with. We all have our blind spots. Regardless of how flexible your mind is, or how skilled you are as a communicator, you are going to have some situations and some relationships that you find challenging. This is the human condition.

➤ *Where and how you get stuck is highly personal.* Things that are hard for you are easy for me, and vice versa. We all have our strengths and flaws, our well-developed skills and our weaknesses. Thus, certain situations may be forever challenging for you, even though they are easy for others. Don't condemn yourself; try to work on developing the mental and emotional "muscles" for navigating those situations that are difficult for you.

▷ *It may take effort to define the problem.* The essence of feeling stuck is that you simply don't know what to do. Finding a solution in stuck situations is not like solving a math problem. If you have to solve an arithmetic equation, the problem is easily defined. The numbers have certain values, all the information is on the page, and you know what you need to solve for. But in stuck situations, sometimes it takes time and effort just to figure out what the problem is and why it's so challenging. Because communication is highly personal, there's a lot of untangling that needs to be done when you assess the situation. Looking at your situation from a variety of perspectives will help you clarify the various factors at play.

▷ *There's not always a clear or objectively correct solution.* To continue the metaphor, getting out of stuck situations is also not like solving a math problem, where there is only one correct answer. There is no single "right" way to address a stuck situation. Don't get frustrated if after identifying the problem, it takes time for you to figure out how you want to handle it.

▷ *Flexing your mind helps generate different options for how to respond.* There are going to be times when you lose your balance; flexing your mind is a way to regain your balance. Often slowing down and refocusing on flexing your mind will be enough to get you going on your own. Other times you may need an outsider to help you do it. But this is a recipe that will give you something to try when you don't know what to do. One benefit of looking at your situation from different and even competing perspectives is that you are free to play out various solutions. Role-playing those solutions may give you clarity about how you want to proceed.

▷ *Momentarily adopting a different perspective doesn't mean you will or should lose your own.* Whether you are the type of person to stubbornly cling to your position at all costs, or the type who is easily swayed by someone else's thinking (or perhaps you fall somewhere in between those two extremes), try to toggle between your own story and the ones generated by looking at the situation from different points of view. Your side is a critical piece of the story, too.

▷ *The solution needs to conform to your own style and circumstances.* Once you've flexed your mind and decided on a course of action, you still have to put your solution into practice in a way that is consistent with your style and personality. Inspiration and education can come from other people, but to be effective, what you ultimately say and how you say it must come from inside you.

▷ *You can always get unstuck.* Although challenges are inevitable, staying mired in an unworkable situation is not. By unilaterally and actively flexing your mind, you will be able to free yourself—whether through better dialogue, better understanding of the situation, making peace with the status quo, or by deciding that walking away is actually a desirable option.

▷ *You can get better over time.* It helps to practice flexing your mind. Sometimes it will allow you to avoid a stuck situation altogether. I look back at situations that were difficult for me years ago. With time and practice, I have gained experience and achieved greater self-awareness, and many of these situations are now easily managed. For those situations that remain difficult, work hard and get into the practice of maintaining a flexible mind; it can shorten how long you spend stuck in the mud and help you get moving in a positive direction.

Shifting perspective is a workout for the mind. It keeps you flexible and helps you stay in shape for the tough situations that inevitably arise. Learning to tell the other side's story faithfully, to see one's own flaws clearly, and to rise above the personal tension to see the wider system are skills you need to navigate your relationships more nimbly. By working on these basic but difficult skills, you will build up a reserve of strength that will help you grow both personally and professionally.

Notes

CHAPTER TWO—SHIFTING PERSPECTIVE

1. As cited by President Sukarno, in Jussi M. Hanhimaki and Odd Arne Westad, eds., *The Cold War: A History in Documents and Eyewitness Accounts* (Oxford: Oxford University Press, 2004), 350.

CHAPTER THREE—OVERCOME YOUR OWN DEFENSES: TEARING DOWN THE WALLS

1. Chris Argyris, *Overcoming Organizational Defenses: Facilitating Organizational Learning* (Boston: Allyn and Bacon, 1990), 87–89.

2. Scott Plous, *The Psychology of Judgment and Decision Making* (New York: McGraw-Hill, 1993), 233.

3. Leon Festinger, *A Theory of Cognitive Dissonance* (Stanford, CA: Stanford University Press, 1957).

4. W. Keith Campbell and Constantine Sedikides, "Self-Threat Magnifies the Self-Serving Bias: A Meta-Analytic Integration," *Review of General Psychology* 3, no. 1 (1999): 23–43.

5. "Biography for George Burns," *Internet Movie Database,* accessed August 26, 2012, http://www.imdb.com/name/nm0122675/bio.

6. As cited in John Keegan, *The Face of Battle* (New York: Penguin, 1976), 334–335.

7. As cited in Anthony St. Peter, *The Greatest Quotations of All Time* (Bloomington, IN: Xlibris, 2010), 572.

8. As cited in Stephen R. Covey, *The Seven Habits of Highly Effective People: Powerful Lessons in Personal Change,* 2nd ed. (New York: Free Press, 2004), 42.

CHAPTER 4—TELL THEIR STORY: LOOKING THROUGH THEIR EYES

1. See Lee Ross and Andrew Ward, "Naïve Realism: Implications for Social Conflict and Misunderstanding" (working paper no. 48, Stanford Center on Conflict and Negotiation, Stanford University, 1995), accessed August 26, 2012, http://www.mediate.com/GeoffSharp/docs/Naive%20Realism.pdf. The authors discuss the tendency to assume that our own view of reality is the same as other people's view of reality. We assume that our reaction to events is reasonable, that other reasonable people would react the same way, and if they don't, they are probably either lazy or irrational.

2. An earlier version of this example can be found in Donny Ebenstein, "Perspective Analysis: Tools for Shifting Perspective to Increase Effectiveness," *OD Practitioner* 39, no. 4 (2007): 22–26. I thank the editors of that journal for their helpful comments.

CHAPTER FIVE—LOOKING FROM THE OUTSIDE IN: SEEING IS BELIEVING

1. An earlier version of this example can be found in Donny Ebenstein, "Perspective Analysis: Tools for Shifting Perspec-

tive to Increase Effectiveness," *OD Practitioner* 39, no. 4 (2007): 22–26.

2. Marshall Goldsmith, *What Got You Here Won't Get You There: How Successful People Become Even More Successful* (New York: Hyperion, 2007).

3. "The Lip Reader," *Seinfeld*, NBC, first aired October 28, 1993.

CHAPTER SIX—DON'T TAKE IT PERSONALLY: UNDERSTANDING IT'S NOT ABOUT YOU

1. An earlier version of this example can be found in Donny Ebenstein, "Perspective Analysis: Tools for Shifting Perspective to Increase Effectiveness," *OD Practitioner* 39, no. 4 (2007): 22–26.

2. Lee Ross, "The Intuitive Psychologist and His Shortcomings: Distortions in the Attribution Process," in *Advances in Experimental Social Psychology*, vol. 10, ed. Leonard Berkowitz (New York: Academic Press 1977), 173–220.

CHAPTER NINE—WHAT COMES NEXT: MAKING CHANGE HAPPEN AND IDENTIFYING DEAD ENDS

1. As cited in John Blaydes, *The Educator's Book of Quotes* (Thousand Oaks, CA: Corwin Press, 2003), 136.

Index